THE HOLLYWOOD CONNECTION

If you're hooked on Hollywood, you're guaranteed a new high on every page of the book that offers lavish and loving lists of:

—Actors and actresses, old and new, famous and forgotten

—Movie titles and roles you'll relish remembering

—Cinema triumphs and disasters

—Endless delightful details and exquisite oddities of the very real world of celluloid make-believe, and all the wonderful nonsense and stirring sense of wonder it creates

THE SECOND SIGNET BOOK OF MOVIE LISTS

Brain teasers from SIGNET

THE SECOND SIGNET

BOOK

OF

MOVIE

LISTS

JEFF ROVIN

A SIGNET BOOK

NEW AMERICAN LIBRARY

TIMES MIRROR

Photo Credits: Insert photos courtesy Paramount Pictures;
20th Century-Fox; Warner Bros.; ABC-TV; Columbia;
Simon Film Productions; Universal; MGM; Museum of Modern
Art/Film Stills Archive; United Artists; Titan Productions;
Walt Disney Productions.

SIGNET TRADEMARK REG. U.S. PAT. OFF. AND FOREIGN COUNTRIES
REGISTERED TRADEMARK—MARCA REGISTRADA
HECHO EN CHICAGO, U.S.A.

SIGNET, SIGNET CLASSICS, MENTOR, PLUME, MERIDIAN AND NAL
BOOKS are published by The New American Library, Inc.,
1633 Broadway, New York, New York 10019

First Printing, May, 1982

1   2   3   4   5   6   7   8   9

PRINTED IN THE UNITED STATES OF AMERICA

ACKNOWLEDGMENTS

For continued assistance in grappling with the output of Hollywood, the author would like to salute Nan Leonard and Dennis Higgins of United Artists; Marc Gerber of MGM; Fredell Pogodin of Universal Pictures; Roberta Burrows at Warner Brothers; Susan Pile at Paramount; Twentieth Century-Fox's Saul Cooper and Ellen Pasternack; the diligent Bill Latham at Walt Disney Productions; Jerry Juroe of Eon Productions Ltd.; Janine Leonard of Avco Embassy; Bill Edwards of CIC in London; Lou Scheimer of Filmation Associates; editorially, appreciation is tendered to Senior Editor Bob Haynie of NAL and agent Jim Trupin.

INTRODUCTION

Welcome to the all-new, all-original *Second Signet Book of Movie Lists*. "Truth needs no flowers of speech," wrote Pope, and this book is just that: one hundred unadorned, often unflattering collections of truisms about the movie industry. Well-known celebrities were consulted for their favorite films; mountains of data were accumulated. The result is, we think, a more detailed, more eclectic volume than the first book.

And, we believe, a lot more fun.

Hope you agree.

Jeff Rovin

THE SECOND SIGNET BOOK OF MOVIE LISTS

SCIENCE AFFECTION

Celebrities choose their favorite science-fiction films:

LILY TOMLIN
1. *The Man in the White Suit* (1952) ("It's brilliant. I love it!")
2. *The Day the Earth Stood Still* (1951)
3. *Rodan* (1957)

CHRISTOPHER REEVE
1. *Close Encounters of the Third Kind* (1977) ("Two-thirds of a very good film. Where it went wrong was Richard Dreyfuss chopping up the living room to make a mud pie. It was also a drastic mistake to show the little munchkins coming out of the spaceship. It limited peoples' imagination to show these little play-dough people.")
2. *The Blob* (1958) ("I really get a kick out of it.")
3. *Breaking the Sound Barrier* (1952)

NEIL SIMON
1. *Star Wars* (1977) ("The most interesting of all, because it had some humor to it.")
2. *Close Encounters of the Third Kind* (1977) ("Mostly from a technological point of view.")
3. *The Thing* (1951) ("I'm really a big fan of that one.")
4. *Invasion of the Body Snatchers* (1956)

CLIFF ROBERTSON
1. *Things to Come* (1936)
2. *The Invisible Man* (1933)
3. *Flash Gordon* (1936)
4. *Planet of the Apes* (1968)

5. *2001: A Space Odyssey* (1968) ("For its special effects, not as far as the narrative is concerned.")

CHEVY CHASE

1. *2001: A Space Odyssey* ("Kubrick did it best and no one has done it as well since.")
2. *Star Wars* ("The sound in space bothered me, though. There's no sound out there! Having watched the moon shots, and even Mercury, Gemini, and the early Apollo flights, we *know* that! But for pure entertainment and excitement, it's quite good.")
3. *The Man in the White Suit* ("That's a beaut!")
4. *Destination Moon*
5. *Diabolique*
6. *War of the Worlds* ("Though it was a little too Americanized, and had too many funny sounds.")

JOHN HOUSEMAN

1. *Close Encounters of the Third Kind* ("Quite interesting and intelligent and well made.")

ROBERT CULP

1. *King Kong*
2. *The Day the Earth Stood Still*
3. *Invasion of the Body Snatchers* (original)
4. *When Worlds Collide*
5. *War of the Worlds*
6. *The Thing*
7. *Them!*

REAGAN'S FOREBEARS

The following Presidents of the United States were only *impersonated* by actors:

George Washington in *Unconquered* (1947) by Richard Gaines

John Adams in *1776* (1972) by William Daniels

Thomas Jefferson in *The Howards of Virginia* (1940) by Richard Carlson

Andrew Jackson in *The President's Lady* (1953) by Charlton Heston

Abraham Lincoln in *Abe Lincoln in Illinois* (1940) by Raymond Massey

Ulysses S. Grant in *The Legend of the Lone Ranger* (1981) by Jason Robards

Grover Cleveland in *Buffalo Bill and the Indians* (1976) by Pat McCormick

Teddy Roosevelt in *The Wind and the Lion* (1975) by Brian Keith

Woodrow Wilson in *Wilson* (1944) by Alexander Knox

Franklin Delano Roosevelt in *Sunrise at Campobello* (1960) by Ralph Bellamy

Harry Truman in *Give 'Em Hell, Harry* (1975) by James Whitmore

John F. Kennedy in *PT 109* (1963) by Cliff Robertson

Andrew Johnson in *Tennessee Johnson* (1942) by Van Heflin

HOT HEIRS

Whenever a movie is a hit, there's bound to be a sequel. Unfortunately a character who has been killed or disposed of in the first film can't always be revived. Hence, his, her, or its progeny are introduced. Here, then, are filmdom's best-known "Son of . . ." pictures:

Son of the Sheik (1926)
Son of Kong (1933)
Son of Frankenstein (1939)
Son of Monte Cristo (1940)
Son of Dracula (1943)
Son of Lassie (1945)
Son of Dr. Jekyll (1951)
Son of Paleface (1952)
Son of Ali Baba (1952)
Son of Belle Starr (1953)
Son of Sinbad (1955)
Son of Robin Hood (1959)
Son of Spartacus (1962)
Son of Capt. Blood (1962)
Son of Flubber (1963)
Son of Godzilla (1969)
Son of Blob (1972)
. . . and a few daughters:
Dracula's Daughter (1936)
Daughter of Rosie O'Grady (1950)
Daughter of Dr. Jekyll (1957)
Frankenstein's Daughter (1959)

PARDON US!

Leading actors and directors select the worst motion pictures they've made:

Charlton Heston: *The Call of the Wild* (1972)
Burt Lancaster: *Airport* (1970)
Paul Newman: *The Silver Chalice* (1954)
Mel Brooks: *High Anxiety* (1977) ("It was too confining for my craziness.")
Gregory Peck: *Only the Valiant* (1951)
Tony Randall: *The Seven Faces of Dr. Lao* (1964) ("The worst padding and dross!")
Max von Sydow: *Exorcist II: The Heretic* (1977)
Stanley Kubrick: *Spartacus* (1960)
John Travolta: *Moment by Moment* (1978)

COUNTDOWN!

Just for fun, a few cardinal films:

15 Malden Lane (1936)
14 Hours (1951)
13 Ghosts (1960)
12 to the Moon (1960)
11 Harrowhouse (1974)
10 Commandments (1956)
9 Hours to Rama (1963)
8 Iron Men (1952)
7 Days in May (1964)
6 Black Horses (1962)
5 Easy Pieces (1970)
4 Horsemen of the Apocalypse (1962)
3 Worlds of Gulliver (1959)
2 for the Seesaw (1962)
One Flew Over the Cuckoo's Nest (1975)
Zero Hour! (1957)

CAMEOS

Films featuring soon-to-be-well-known actors and actresses in little-known or anonymous parts:

Waikiki Wedding (1937)
   Anthony Quinn as an Hawaiian named Kimo.
A Star Is Born (1937)
   Lana Turner as an unbilled extra.
The Return of Dr. X (1937)
   Humphrey Bogart as the mad scientist Dr. Xavier.
The Thing (1951)
   James Arness, years before he became Matt Dillon on TV's *Gunsmoke,* played the alien vampire—a vegetable in humanoid form!
Captain Horatio Hornblower (1951)
   Christopher Lee, prior to donning cape and fangs as Dracula, played a Spanish officer.
Zombies of the Stratosphere (1952)
   Leonard Nimoy—Mr. Spock of television's *Star Trek*—first played an alien named Narab in this movie serial.
Quo Vadis (1951)
   Sophia Loren appeared as a scantily clad extra.
I Was a Teenage Werewolf (1957)
   Michael Landon, before striking gold on *Bonanza* and *Little House on the Prairie,* was moonstruck in this popular horror film.
The Blob (1958)
   Steve McQueen as a brash youngster.
Teenage Caveman (1959)
   Robert Vaughn, in garb far different from his yet-to-come *Man from U.N.C.L.E.* days.

CAMEOS (continued)

The Magic Christian (1970)
   Yul Brynner, in drag, singing "Mad About the Boy."
The Adventure of Sherlock Holmes' Smarter Brother (1975)
   Albert Finney as a face in a theatre crowd.
Dante's Inferno (1935)
   Rita Hayworth as a writhing soul in torment.

COMIC RELIEF

Theatrical, live-action motion pictures based on the exploits of characters who originated in the comic-strip medium:

Dream of a Rarebit Fiend (1906)
Tailspin Tommy (1934)
Palooka (1934)
Tailspin Tommy and the Great Air Mystery (1935)
Ace Drummond (1936)
Flash Gordon (1936)
Dick Tracy (1937)
Jungle Jim (1937)
Secret Agent X–9 (1937)
Tim Tyler's Luck (1937)
Dick Tracy Returns (1938)
Flash Gordon's Trip to Mars (1938)
Blondie (twenty-eight films made between 1938–1951)
Dick Tracy's G-men (1939)
Mandrake the Magician (1939)
Little Orphan Annie (1939)
Terry and the Pirates (1940)
Flash Gordon Conquers the Universe (1940)
Dick Tracy vs. Crime Inc. (1941)
Don Winslow of the Navy (1942)
The Phantom (1943)
Adventures of Smilin' Jack (1943)
Secret Agent X-9 (1945)
Brenda Starr, Reporter (1945)
Brick Bradford (1947)
Bruce Gentry, Daredevil of the Skies (1949)
Prince Valiant (1954)

COMIC RELIEF (continued)

Sad Sack (1957)
L'il Abner (1959)
Dondi (1961)
Friday Foster (1975)
Popeye (1980)
Flash Gordon (1980)
Annie (1982)

. . . and comic books:

The Adventures of Captain Marvel (1941)
Spy Smasher (1942)
Batman (1943)
Captain America (1944)
Superman (1948)
Batman and Robin (1949)
Atom Man vs. Superman (1950)
Superman and the Mole Men (1951)
Blackhawk (1952)
Batman (1966)
Tales from the Crypt (1971)
The Vault of Horror (1972)
Superman (1978)
Superman II (1981)
Swamp Thing (1982)

THOSE AMAZING MONSTERS!

The ten most unusual beasts in cinema history:

Robot Monster (1953)
 A space-helmeted gorilla from the stars.
Forbidden Planet (1956)
 An invisible monster from a scientist's id roams the planet Altair-Four and tears people apart.
The Monolith Monsters (1957)
 Space rocks grow huge and reproduce, attacking people and turning them to stone.
The Unknown Terror (1957)
 Fungus monsters hide in a cave. . . .
The Brain from Planet Arous (1958)
 Actually, *two* brains—one a villain and the other a law-brain, both from a distant world.
The Fly (1958)
 While experimenting with matter-transmission, a scientist mingles his atoms with those of a fly; he ends up with the fly's head and arm, the fly with his.
Angry Red Planet (1959)
 A giant martian bat-crab-rat-spider is the highlight of this improbable adventure.
Invasion of the Star Creatures (1964)
 Carrot beings from space.
Godzilla vs. the Smog Monster (1972)
 The latter creature is named Hedorah, and is made of living pollution.
The Golden Voyage of Sinbad (1973)
 But one of the many creatures that menace Sinbad is his ship's masthead, which rips itself from the prow and goes on a murderous rampage.

COMEBACKS!

Just when you thought they were washed up, with a trail of flops behind them, these ten stars came back like the pros they are, with popular or world-class performances:

Peter O'Toole in *The Stunt Man* (1980): After years of drought, which included such misfires as *Man Friday* (1976), O'Toole won himself an Oscar nomination.

Burt Lancaster in *Atlantic City* (1981): A great performer who hadn't had a theatrical hit since *Airport* (1970) gave one of the finest performances of his career.

Marlon Brando in *The Godfather* (1972): He was shunned after his exploits on films like *Mutiny on the Bounty* (1962) allegedly drove up their budgets and caused tempers to bubble over.

Errol Flynn in *The Sun Also Rises* (1957): The swash-buckler finally switched from action roles, for which he'd become too starchy, and played a drunk.

Lily Tomlin in *Nine-to-Five* (1980): Her career had been decimated due to *Moment by Moment* (1978), but she was in brilliant comedic form for this runaway hit.

Farrah Fawcett in *The Cannonball Run* (1981): Destroyed by three strikeouts in three times at bat, she rose phoenixlike in this Burt Reynolds film.

Richard Burton in *Equus* (1979): Though the film wasn't successful, Burton's Oscar nomination restored credibility to a career debilitated by such disasters as *The Klansman* (1974) and *Exorcist II: The Heretic*.

George Hamilton in *Love at First Bite* (1979): He recovered in grand style as Dracula, after nearly a decade of decay capped by *Evel Knievel* (1972).

Peter Sellers in *Return of the Pink Panther* (1975): The comic genius of the early 1960s faded late in the decade, though his career was revitalized by his return to the role of Inspector Clouseau.

Mickey Rooney in *The Black Stallion* (1979): Overlooked for decades, Rooney returned in a big way with an Oscar nomination for this hit film.

. . . and a few talented performers who *will* be back on top:

Cliff Robertson	Frank Langella
Elliot Gould	

SECONDS

A few sequels which flopped at the box office:

Son of Kong (1933): Though not a bad little picture, it was rushed out to cash in on the enormous success of *King Kong*, and paled in comparison.

The Unseen (1945): An unsuccessful followup to the hit ghost film of 1944 *The Uninvited*.

Return to Peyton Place (1961): Lacking the stellar cast of the original 1957 soap opera, and coming too many years later, the film did not attract its audience.

One More Time (1970): Despite good direction by Jerry Lewis, this sequel to the comedy *Salt and Pepper* of two years previous did not woo theatergoers.

Son of Blob (1972): Directed by Larry Hagman, this camp film was funny only to science-fiction fans, who like their S-F straight; hence, no market!

Exorcist II: The Heretic (1977): John Boorman went on to direct *Excalibur,* thereby redeeming himself after this silly sequel to the 1973 occult smash.

Force Ten from Navarone (1978): More macho heroics, without the charisma of the original cast of Gregory Peck and David Niven. One of Robert Shaw's last two films.

Return of a Man Called Horse (1976): Not a bad picture at all, just unrecognized. A sequel to the 1970 film, both starred Richard Harris.

Empire of the Ants (1977): H. G. Wells never had it so bad as first *Food of the Gods* was murdered in 1976, and then his sequel to same a year later.

More American Graffiti (1979): George Lucas should have let it lay, this sequel to his 1973 hit giving him one of his two box-office flops. (The other was his first film, the intriguing *THX-1138* made in 1971.)

Butch and Sundance: The Early Years (1979): A quieter, less leering film than the picture, made a decade earlier, which inspired this "prequel."

Beyond the Poseidon Adventure (1980): How Irwin Allen could miss so terribly in this sequel to his 1972 disaster epic is mystifying. Sunk with nary a trace.

Nine stars who have bared more than their souls in motion pictures:

Charlton Heston running naked through the underbrush in *Planet of the Apes* (1968)

Jane Fonda undraped in *Barbarella* (1968)

Kirk Douglas barebottom in *Saturn III* (1980)

Jill Clayburgh in the midst of lovemaking in *An Unmarried Woman* (1978)

Adam West let down his guard, along with his pants, for *The Happy Hooker Goes to Hollywood* (1979)

Valerie Perrine went nude in the part of a stripper for *Lenny* (1974)

Oliver Reed exposed all in *Women in Love* (1970)

Sissy Spacek offered full frontal nudity in *Carrie* (1976)

Julie Andrews went topless in *S.O.B.* (1981)

AUTHOR! AUTHOR!

Lest we forget, among the fifty most profitable films of all time, fourteen were based on books:

Jaws (1975) #3
The Exorcist (1973) #5
The Godfather (1972) #6
Gone With the Wind (1939) #13
Kramer vs. Kramer (1979) #17
One Flew Over the Cuckoo's Nest (1975) #18
The Towering Inferno (1975) #25
Dr. Zhivago (1965) #28
Airport (1970) #30
Mary Poppins (1964) #32
The Poseidon Adventure (1972) #36
Ben-Hur (1959) #47
Coal Miner's Daughter (1980) #49
The Amityville Horror (1979) #50

SCIENCE FACTION

Films about real-life scientists:

Dr. Ehrlich's Magic Bullet (1940): Edward G. Robinson conquers venereal disease.

The Story of Louis Pasteur (1936): Paul Muni won an Oscar fighting hoof-and-mouth.

The Story of Alexander Graham Bell (1939): Don Ameche phones in a fine performance.

Young Tom Edison (1940): Mickey Rooney stands tall in the title role.

Edison, the Man (1940): This time it's Spencer Tracy who sees the light.

Madame Curie (1943): Greer Garson and radium.

The Great Moment (1944): Joel McCrea invents anesthesia.

The Beginning or the End (1947): The Manhattan Project, starring Hume Cronyn as Dr. Oppenheimer, Ludwig Stossel as Albert Einstein, and Joseph Calleia as Enrico Fermi.

Breaking the Sound Barrier (1952): Though this film is about no one researcher in particular, its composite portrait of pilots and engineers who flew faster than sound is intensely accurate.

I Aim at the Stars (1960): The saga of rocket scientist Werner Von Braun.

The Darwin Adventure (1972): Nicholas Clay as the famed Father of Evolution.

Galileo (1974): Israeli actor Chaim Topol in the title role.

Freud (1962): Montgomery Clift as the man behind the id.

The Magic Box (1951): Robert Donat as William Friese-Greene, the man who invented the moving picture.

NARCISSISM

The following are film-production companies founded by celebrities to produce more personally satisfying pictures:

Eltee Productions: Lana Turner
Bryna Company: Kirk Douglas
Norlan Productions: Burt Lancaster
Malpaso Productions: Clint Eastwood
Batjac Productions: John Wayne
Atticus Corporation: Gregory Peck
IPC Films: Jane Fonda
Dogwood Productions: Warren Beatty
Big Stick Productions: Michael Douglas
Deliverance Productions: Burt Reynolds
Essex Productions: Frank Sinatra
Beckworth Productions: Rita Hayworth

UNCLE SAM WANTS YOU!

A few films which "rank" with the best:

Captain Horatio Hornblower (1951)
Major Dundee (1965)
Sgt. York (1941)
Buck Privates (1941)
The General Died at Dawn (1936)
The Horizontal Lieutenant (1962)
The Admiral Was a Lady (1950)
Colonel Blimp (1943)

The following films featured main characters who wore patches:

Escape from New York (1981): Snake Plisskin, played by Kurt Russell

Thunderball (1965): Largo, James Bond's nemesis, played by Adolfo Celi

The Three Musketeers (1974): Rochefort, the assassin, played by Christopher Lee

The Vikings (1958): Einar, played by Kirk Douglas, who loses his eye midway through the film thanks to Eric (Tony Curtis)

Castle Keep (1969): Burt Lancaster's quixotic major

True Grit (1969): John Wayne as Rooster Cogburn

YOU'RE FIRED!

Movies in which the story featured a prominent blaze:

In Old Chicago (1938): Mrs. O'Leary's cow strikes
Gone With the Wind (1939): Atlanta reduced to ashes
Quo Vadis (1951): Nero fiddles through one of history's worst fires
The Blazing Forest (1952): Holocaust in the domain of Smokey the Bear
Ring of Fire (1961): More burning woodland
Barabbas (1962): Rome's still aflame
Hellfighters (1969): Duke Wayne vs. oil fires
Firechasers (1970): Arsonist on the loose
The Towering Inferno (1974): A San Francisco skyscraper burns, all 124 stories of it
Circus World (1964): A bigtop blaze which, in reality, nearly cost star John Wayne his life.

It's an axiom of filmmaking that actors, as a rule, can't make a successful transition from television to motion pictures. While it's true that many have tried and failed, a few have made the jump:

James Garner: From 1957 to 1960, this actor became closely identified with the character of Bret Maverick in the ABC western *Maverick*. Yet, he was able to gain instant acceptance on the screen in *The Great Escape* (1963) and *Grand Prix* (1966), and has moved freely from one medium to the other.

Sally Field: She was TV's Sister Bertrille from 1967–1970, but in movies like *Smokey and the Bandit* (1977) and *Norma Rae* (1979)—the latter of which won her the best-actress Oscar—she proved she can straddle the media with ease.

John Travolta: Quite possibly the most impressive jump of all, going from one TV series, *Welcome Back, Kotter*, where he played Vinnie Barbarino, to an Oscar-nominated performance in *Saturday Night Fever* (1977).

Steve McQueen: Another dramatic jump, as McQueen went from three years of *Wanted: Dead or Alive* to films like *The Great Escape* and *Bullitt* (1968). He was asking $5,000,000 per film at the time of his death in 1980.

Clint Eastwood: Eastwood went from *Rawhide* (1959–1966) as Rowdy Yates, to Italy for "Spaghetti westerns," then returned to America a superstar.

Burt Reynolds: His series' *Hawk* (1966) and *Dan August* (1970) were unsuccessful, and Reynolds turned to motion pictures. The rest, as they say, is history. Both series were subsequently rebroadcast to far stronger ratings than they originally earned.

Richard Chamberlain: After being type-cast as *Dr. Kildare* from 1961–1966, Chamberlain threw himself into such meaty stage roles as Hamlet, and distinguished himself in motion pictures such as *The Three Musketeers* (1974) and *The Last Wave* (1979). Like James Garner, he now moves freely between the media.

Alan Alda: Thanks to *M*A*S*H*, the actor had a forum from which to launch a successful film career which has thus far included *The Seduction of Joe Tynan* (1979), *The Four Seasons* (1981), and others.

Goldie Hawn: A scatterbrained dancer/comedienne on TV, she became an actress of surprising range in motion pictures like *Cactus Flower* (1969), which won her an Oscar, *The Sugarland Express* (1974), and *Private Benjamin* (1980).

Roger Moore: He was TV's *The Saint*, and before that had starred in *Maverick*, *The Alaskans*, *The Persuaders*, and others. Then he became James Bond, and apart from the five 007 features has made many other films.

Bruce Lee: After only one season as Kato on *The Green Hornet*, the martial-arts expert became the dominant force in the "chop-socky" films until his death.

Art Carney: For 16 years he was Ed Norton on *The Honeymooners*. Moving into motion pictures, he won an Oscar for *Harry and Tonto* (1974), and has added weight and class to many otherwise mild films such as *Sunburn* (1979).

SUPERLATIVES!!

Hollywood is known for its bigger-than-life stars—but how about some of those titles?

The Greatest Story Ever Told (1965)
The Best Little Whorehouse in Texas (1982)
The Magnificent Seven (1960)
The Fabulous World of Jules Verne (1961)
The Incredible Shrinking Woman (1980)
The Amazing Dobermans (1976)
The Astounding She-Monster (1958)
Fantastic Voyage (1966)
The Miraculous Journey (1948)
More Than a Miracle (1967)
The Towering Inferno (1974)

UNSAVORY CHARACTERS

People so nasty that viewers were warned of their perfidy in the title itself:

The Notorious Landlady (1962)
The Awful Dr. Orloff (1961)
The Terrible People (1960)
The Horrible Dr. Hichcock (1962)
The Wicked Woman (1954)
The Mad Ghoul (1943)
The Savage Seven (1968)
Brute Man (1946)
The Deadly Companions (1961)
Bloody Mama (1970)
The Most Dangerous Man Alive (1961)

Actors who badly wanted certain roles, some of whom got them and some who did not:

Charlton Heston: Two roles eluded the Oscar-winning star, that of Thomas More in *A Man for All Seasons* (1966)—because Paul Scofield had created the part on the stage ("And was excellent," Heston concedes)—and Sheriff Brody in *Jaws* (1975) because Heston had just completed *Earthquake* (1974) and *Airport 1975* (1974), and Universal felt that a third jeopardy film would be a helpless self-parody.

Frank Sinatra: The part of Maggio in *From Here to Eternity* (1953) went to him only after Eli Wallach dropped out and Sinatra agreed to do the movie for a pittance. He won an Oscar.

Burt Lancaster: Along with Ernest Borgnine and every other actor in Hollywood, he wanted the part of *The Godfather* (1972). Brando got it when he did a screen test and director Francis Coppola begged to have him.

Peter Sellers: Producer George Pal wanted him for *The Seven Faces of Dr. Lao* (1964), as all seven faces—including Medusa, Pan, Lao, *et al.*—but Tony Randall was under contract and MGM gave him the part. He was superb.

Donald O'Connor: Again, George Pal and the star wanted one another for *tom thumb* (1958), but MGM wanted their contract player Russ Tamblyn. He, too, was excellent.

Bette Davis: There was no end to the number of actresses who coveted the role of Scarlett O'Hara in *Gone With the Wind* (1939), but none more than Ms. Davis.

However, Warner Brothers would put up the money only if Errol Flynn co-starred as Rhett. Ms. Davis refused, and the film went to MGM.

Shirley Temple: Whether or not the child wanted to play Dorothy in *The Wizard of Oz* (1939), MGM wanted her. It is rumored the studio offered to loan Temple's bosses at 20th Century-Fox Clark Gable and Jean Harlow for Ms. Temple, but the death of the latter ended that deal.

LIKE FATHER, LIKE SON ...
AND DAUGHTER

The children of noted actors who have remained in the profession:

Douglas Fairbanks, Jr.
Lon Chaney, Jr.
Patrick Wayne (son of John)
Taryn Power (daughter of Tyrone)
Adam Arkin (son of Alan)
Michael Douglas (son of Kirk)
Keith Carradine (son of John)
Geraldine Chaplin (daughter of Charlie)
Keenan Wynn (son of Ed)
Chris Lemmon (son of Jack)
Robert Walker, Jr.
Vanessa and Lynn Redgrave (daughters of Michael)
Hayley Mills (daughter of John)
Jamie Lee Curtis (daughter of Tony and Janet Leigh)

... plus some one-time-only appearances:

Will Lancaster (son of Burt) in *The Midnight Man* (1974)

Fraser Heston (son of Charlton) in *The Ten Commandments* (1956) (as the baby Moses)

Sean Flynn (son of Errol) in *The Son of Captain Blood* (1962)

Harold Lloyd, Jr., in *Frankenstein's Daughter* (1959)

DYNAMIC DUOS

Husband-and-wife actors (plus a few live-ins), most still married and still acting

Jessica Tandy and Hume Cronyn
Farrah Fawcett and Ryan O'Neal
Mia Farrow and Woody Allen
Paul Newman and Joanne Woodward
Cliff Robertson and Dina Merrill
Mel Brooks and Anne Bancroft
Patty Duke and John Astin
Gena Rowlands and John Cassavetes

... and a few from the past:

Natalie Wood and Robert Wagner
Laurence Olivier and Vivien Leigh
Ronald Reagan and Jane Wyman
Douglas Fairbanks, Sr., and Mary Pickford
George Burns and Gracie Allen
William Holden and Stephanie Powers
Frank Sinatra and Ava Gardner
Lex Barker and Lana Turner
Tyrone Power and Linda Christian
Elizabeth Taylor and Richard Burton
Cary Grant and Dyan Cannon
Frank Sinatra and Mia Farrow
Tony Curtis and Janet Leigh
Shirley Jones and Jack Cassidy
Clark Gable and Carole Lombard
Humphrey Bogart and Lauren Bacall
John Derek and Ursula Andress (note: though Derek is presently married to actress Bo, he is a retired actor)

DYNAMIC DUOS (continued)

Jason Robards and Lauren Bacall
Joan Crawford and Franchot Tone
Susan Strasberg and Christopher Jones
Bette Davis and Gary Merrill
Shelley Winters and Vittorio Gassman
Orson Welles and Rita Hayworth
John Ireland and Joanne Dru
Mickey Rooney and Ava Gardner
Esther Williams and Fernando Lamas
George Sanders and Zsa Zsa Gabor
Steve McQueen and Ali MacGraw
Lupe Velez and Johnny Weissmuller
Elsa Lanchester and Charles Laughton
George Peppard and Elizabeth Ashley
Robert Taylor and Barbara Stanwyck

Freeing classic ad lines from the limbo of long-gone motion pictures:

"Makes *Ben-Hur* Look Like an Epic!" *Monty Python and the Holy Grail* (1974)

"More Entertaining than Humanly Possible" *The Muppet Movie* (1978)

"You'll Believe a Man Can Fly!" *Superman* (1978)

"The Human Adventure Is Just Beginning!" *Star Trek: The Motion Picture* (1979)

"In Space, No One Can Hear You Scream" *Alien* (1979)

"Even in Space—The Ultimate Enemy Is Man" *Outland* (1981)

"Zany, Zexy, Zensational!" *Zorro, the Gay Blade* (1981)

"They Can Tear the Scream from Your Throat!" *Wolfen* (1981)

"A Step Beyond Science Fiction" *Heavy Metal* (1981)

"Mirror, Mirror on the Wall, Who's the Murderer Among Them All?" *Agatha Christie's The Mirror Crack'd* (1980)

"The Story of the Longest-run Date in the History of Non-marriage" *Same Time Next Year* (1979)

"What One Loves About Life Are the Things That Fade" *Heaven's Gate* (1980)

"No Mortal Could Possess It. No Kingdom Could Command It. Behold . . . *Excalibur*" (1980)

"Advertising Is a Serious Game. Now, It's a Deadly One at the *Agency*" (1980)

"It's Saturday. The Boys Are Playing a Little Game. The Winner Gets to Live" *The Double McGuffin* (1980)

"He Thinks Someone Is Trying to Kill Him. He's Dead Right." *Last Embrace* (1979)

"This Is the Way It Was" *One Million Years B.C.* (1966) (starring Raquel Welch)

"From Out of Space . . . a Warning and an Ultimatum!" *The Day the Earth Stood Still* (1951)

"Ravishing a Universe for Love" *Mothra* (1962)

"The Creature Created by Man and Forgotten by Nature" *The Curse of Frankenstein* (1957)

"*Westworld* . . . Where Nothing Can Possibly Go Wrong" (1973)

"The Spaced Out Odyssey" *Dark Star* (1974)

"Being the Adventures of a Young Man Whose Principal Interests Are Rape, Ultra-violence and Beethoven" *A Clockwork Orange* (1971)

"Somewhere in the Universe, There Must Be Something Better than Man" *Planet of the Apes* (1968)

"To Love a Stranger Is Easy. To Kill a Lover Is Not." *Eye of the Needle* (1981)

"The 8th Wonder of the Screen" *The 7th Voyage of Sinbad* (1958)

"They're Too Wild for One World!" *Abbott and Costello Go to Mars* (1953)

"A Monster Science Created but Could Not Destroy!" *Frankenstein* (1931)

"Murder Has a Sound All of Its Own" *Blow Out* (1981)

"Two Heads Are Better than One" *Cheech & Chong's Nice Dreams* (1981)

"The Only Thing Straight in This Movie Is . . . the Jacket" *Cheech & Chong's Nice Dreams*

"What Would *You* Have Done if You Had Been Given Absolute Power of Life and Death Over Everybody Else in the Whole World?" *Caligula* (1979)

"People Used to Laugh at Eric Binford . . . Now With

Every Performance He Knocks Them Dead" *Fade to Black* (1980)

"There Was Only One Thing More Terrifying than Leaving the House . . . Staying in It!" *Phobia* (1979)

"Finally, a Movie You Can Sink Your Teeth Into . . ." *Lunch Wagon* (1980)

"10 Seconds: The Pain Begins. 15 Seconds: You Can't Breathe. 20 Seconds: Your Head Explodes" *Scanners* (1980)

"Once He Gets You Inside the Hearse, You're Better Off Dead!" *The Hearse* (1980)

"Perseguido, Odiado, La Vida de un Delator . . ." *La Muerte del Soplón* (1978)

BETTE DAVIS' FAVORITE FILMS

1. *The Best Years of Our Lives* (1946)
2. *Mrs. Miniver* (1942) ("Oh boy, boy, boy, that was something else!")
3. *The Old Man and the Sea* (1958) ("That performance of Spencer's—God!")
4. *Camille* (1936) ("I'll never forget it.")
5. *Flesh and the Devil* (1927) ("Unbelievable!")
6. *Open City* (1946)
7. *Bellissima* (1951)
8. *Julia* (1977) ("The whole thing, the script and the photography, Jane and Vanessa—they went back to the good old days of moviemaking. A colossal film!")
9. *The Turning Point* (1977) ("That was off in some beautiful world")
10. *The Graduate* (1967) ("Brilliant. Brilliant. That's a great one.")

MANY HAPPY RETURNS

Birthdays of the stars, and for those no longer with us the day on which they died:

Lana Turner: February 8, 1921
Frank Sinatra: December 12, 1915
Judy Garland: June 10, 1922, to June 21, 1969
Kirk Douglas: December 9, 1916
Errol Flynn: June 20, 1909, to October 14, 1959
Bela Lugosi: October 20, 1882, to August 16, 1956
Anthony Quinn: April 15, 1915
Laurence Olivier: May 22, 1907
Burt Lancaster: November 2, 1913
Tyrone Power: May 5, 1914, to November 15, 1958
Elizabeth Taylor: February 27, 1932
Boris Karloff: November 23, 1887, to February 2, 1969
Charlton Heston: October 4, 1923
James Cagney: July 17, 1899
Cary Grant: January 18, 1904
Robert Taylor: August 5, 1911, to June 8, 1969
Clark Gable: February 1, 1901, to November 16, 1960
Humphrey Bogart: January 23, 1899, to January 14, 1957
Shirley MacLaine: April 24, 1934
Sean Connery: September 25, 1930
Vincent Price: May 27, 1911
Joseph Cotten: May 15, 1905
Spencer Tracy: April 5, 1900, to June 11, 1967

COMIN' AT YA!

Movies in which special persons come into a town, and the lives of one or more of its inhabitants are forever changed:

The Rainmaker (1956): Con-artist Burt Lancaster comes to a drought-stricken town in the American Southwest. Though he has trouble performing the titular miracle, his faith in himself builds the self-image of spinster Katharine Hepburn.

The Music Man (1962): Professor Harold Hill (Robert Preston) arrives in turn-of-the-century River City and gives the inhabitants new courage and self-respect.

The Seven Faces of Dr. Lao (1964): An ancient Chinese brings his circus of wonders to the Southwestern town of Abalone at the dawning of the twentieth century. The freaks and seers of the sideshows are reflections of the citizens themselves, forcing them to reassess their own lives.

Bye Bye Birdie (1963): A rock star comes to meet a townful of teen fans, also affecting their stuffy, sneering parents.

A Fistful of Dollars (1966): Rugged Clint Eastwood comes to San Miguel and is caught up in the rivalry of two warring families.

Casablanca (1943): Ilsa Laszlo (Ingrid Bergman) arrives at Richard Blaine's Café Américain, where Rick (Humphrey Bogart) becomes involved with WWII intrigue.

Gulliver's Travels (1939): The English physician, shipwrecked in the little land of Lilliput, ends a war and unites the battling kingdoms.

Superman (1978): The Man of Steel (Christopher Reeve) goes from Krypton to Metropolis and brings romance to Lois Lane (Margot Kidder) while saving two coasts from nuclear demolition.

The Wizard of Oz (1939): Judy Garland visits Oz, slays two witches, exposes a phony sorcerer, and leaves a scarecrow in charge.

Flash Gordon (1980): Quarterback Flash rockets to Mongo and frees its inhabitants from the cruel rule of Emperor Ming—at the same time saving earth from destruction.

Destination Tokyo (1944): Captain Cary Grant sneaks his submarine *Copperfin* into Japanese waters, helping to pave the way for a bombing raid on the Japanese metropolis.

Frisco Kid (1935): Bat Morgan (James Cagney) finds himself in San Francisco and pauses long enough to rise from sailor to rich man.

Boom Town (1940): Clark Gable and Spencer Tracy both arrive in the prosperous oil town and intertwine their destinies irrevocably with those of the inhabitants.

Stagecoach (1939): The Ringo Kid (John Wayne, natch) joins the passengers after their journey is under way, radically affecting the lives of all five.

ACTING DIRECTORS

Noted directors who have starred in films for others:

Otto Preminger in *Stalag 17* (1953)
John Huston in *The Bible* (1966)
Erich von Stroheim in *Sunset Boulevard* (1950)
Cecil B. DeMille in *Sunset Boulevard* (1950)
François Truffaut in *Close Encounters of the Third Kind* (1977)

Films about famous, real-life singers—torch, pop, opera, and otherwise and other musicians:

The Great Caruso (1951) starring Mario Lanza
The Eddie Cantor Story (1953) starring Keefe Brasselle
With a Song in My Heart (1952) starring Susan Hayward as Jane Froman
So This Is Love (1953) starring Kathryn Grayson as opera star Grace Moore
I'll Cry Tomorrow (1956) starring Susan Hayward as Lillian Roth
The Helen Morgan Story (1957) starring Ann Blyth
Lady Sings the Blues (1972) starring Diana Ross as Billie Holliday
Funny Girl (1968) and *Funny Lady* (1975) starring Barbra Streisand as Fanny Brice
The Buddy Holly Story (1978) starring Gary Busey as the pop singer

. . . plus a few musicians and the like:

The Eddy Duchin Story (1956) starring Tyrone Power
The Glenn Miller Story (1953) starring James Stewart
The Benny Goodman Story (1955) starring Steve Allen
The Gene Krupa Story (1959) starring Sal Mineo
The Fabulous Dorseys (1947) starring the fabulous Dorseys themselves!
The Five Pennies (1959) starring Danny Kaye as Red Nichols
Rhapsody in Blue (1945) starring Robert Alda as George Gershwin

ACTING UP A SONG (continued)

St. Louis Blues (1958): Nat King Cole as the blues king W. C. Handy

Scott Joplin (1977): Ragtime pianist played by Billy Dee Williams

Night and Day (1946): Cary Grant played composer Cole Porter.

Interrupted Melody (1955) starring Eleanor Parker as Australian opera singer Marjorie Lawrence.

ERNEST BORGNINE'S FAVORITE FILMS

His own:

Marty (1955)
The Wild Bunch (1969)
Bad Day at Black Rock (1954)
The Poseidon Adventure (1972)
Pay or Die (1960)
From Here to Eternity (1953)

Films made by others:

How Green Was My Valley (1941)
All the King's Men (1949)
"Almost anything old-fashioned in black and white—
where they don't go into bedrooms and slash people."

MICHAEL CAINE'S FAVORITE FILMS

On the Waterfront (1954)
Charade (1963)
The Third Man (1949)

POSTMARK: STARDOM!

The birthplaces of some of our greatest stars:

Doris Day: Cincinnati, Ohio
Alan Arkin: Brooklyn, New York
Lauren Bacall: New York, New York
Joanne Woodward: Thomasville, Georgia
Natalie Wood: San Francisco, California
Tony Curtis: New York, New York
Clint Eastwood: San Francisco, California
Raquel Welch: Chicago, Illinois
Omar Sharif: Alexandria, Egypt
George Segal: Great Neck, Long Island
Glenn Ford: Quebec, Canada
Ava Gardner: Smithfield, North Carolina
James Garner: Norman, Oklahoma
Cliff Robertson: La Jolla, California
Debbie Reynolds: El Paso, Texas
Vincent Price: St. Louis, Missouri
Dustin Hoffman: Los Angeles, California
William Holden: O'Fallon, Illinois
Rock Hudson: Winnetka, Illinois
Sidney Poitier: Miami, Florida
Gregory Peck: La Jolla, California
Kim Novak: Chicago, Illinois
Jack Nicholson: Neptune, New Jersey
Paul Newman: Cleveland, Ohio

WHIPPED!!

Characters famous for speaking softly and carrying a big whip:

Harrison Ford as Indiana Jones in *Raiders of the Lost Ark* (1981), a chap who used his whip not only to beat back opponents, but to haul himself in and out of dangerous places.

Walter Matthau in *The Kentuckian* (1955), playing Burt Lancaster's antagonist and nearly doing him in during a whip fight.

Charles Laughton and Trevor Howard as Captain Bligh in *Mutiny on the Bounty* (1935 and 1962), who, though they did not wield the whip personally, ordered many a sailor's back flayed.

The Adventures of Bullwhip Griffin (1967) promised more than it delivered, whipwise, the film being a comedy from Walt Disney Productions.

Vincent Price as Baka, the master builder, in *The Ten Commandments* (1953). He could flick a fly from his horse's ear without breaking his stride, he was heard to boast. However, before he could ply his talents to the torture of Joshua (John Derek), his back was broken by Moses (Charlton Heston).

George Hamilton as *Zorro, the Gay Blade* (1981), latest in a long line of whip-cracking Don Diegos.

Calibos, satyr in *Clash of the Titans* (1981). This monster, cursed by Zeus, is fond of getting attention by snapping his whip, and also using it to trip mortals who are fleeing for their lives from some incredible monster.

GRIM FAREWELL

Some of the less pleasant ways that characters have perished in motion pictures:

Stephen Boyd as Messala, in *Ben-Hur* (1959), had a chariot crack up beneath him. Still holding the reins, he was dragged by his team of horses along the dirt arena until he was trampled by a pursuing chariot. Yakima Canutt, who staged the race, referred to it as "Making a Messala Burger."

Boris Karloff, as Hjalmar Poelzig in *The Black Cat* (1934), is lashed to a frame and has the skin flayed from his living body by Dr. Vitus Verdegast (Bela Lugosi, natch).

It's not especially novel, though it's savage as any screen death: James Caan, as Sonny Corleone, machine-gunned to ribbons at the toll booth in *The Godfather* (1972).

Though there are many inventive deaths in *Theatre of Blood* (1973), Robert Morley suffers the sickest of them: vengeful actor Edward Lionheart (Vincent Price) kills the puppies of critic Meredith Merridrew (Robert Morley) and, baking them in a stew, force-feeds them to Merridrew until he chokes to death.

Quo Vadis (1951) brought to the screen the unpleasant death of Peter (Finlay Currie), who was not only crucified but crucified upside-down.

As if being burned at the stake were not bad enough, Princess Asa (Barbara Steele) first undergoes the torment of having the spiked mask of Satan hammered onto her face, the reward of the Inquisition for being a devil worshiper in *Black Sunday* (1960)

Here's one that everyone will remember, which doesn't, however, make it any less gruesome: the demise of Quint (Robert Shaw) in *Jaws* (1975), chewed up feet-first by the Great White Shark.

Speaking of the familiar, the melting of witch Margaret Hamilton in *The Wizard of Oz* (1939), though rendered without particularly grotesque embellishments, is nonetheless a gruesome classic.

Adding insult to injury, not only is the evil Grand Vizier Jaffar (Conrad Veidt) shot through the forehead with an arrow in *The Thief of Bagdad* (1940), but the wound causes him to plummet from the back of a flying horse, to be broken on the earth below.

Dracula (1979) managed the impossible: gave the vampire a fresh kind of death. In his time, the monster has been staked, reduced to ash by the sun's rays, impaled on a cross, frozen in a river, and the like. Frank Langella's death was easily the most horrendous. Battling with Dr. Van Helsing (Laurence Olivier) in the hold of a ship, he is impaled on a grapple and hauled, writhing, up the mast of the ship. There, he is slowly incinerated by the purifying daylight.

The Naked Jungle (1953) had a number of people eaten by the savage little ants known as Maribunta—though the most vivid on-screen death is that of the lonely dam-keeper, who falls asleep and forgets to drown out the onrushing army of lethal insects. When he wakes, they're all over him and his lazy bones are picked clean.

It's a quick death, but an unpleasant one: a bold policeman, firing his pistol at a rampaging dinosaur in *The Beast from Twenty Thousand Fathoms* (1953), is snapped up in the jaws of the giant monster. However, he does not die instantly. The creature picks him up by his head, bites down to his torso, and allows him to kick, scream, and squirm for a long moment before swallowing him down.

SEEING DOUBLE

They played twin parts in the same film:

George Hamilton in *Zorro, the Gay Blade* (1981) as brothers

Bette Davis in *Dead Ringer* (1964) as sisters

Peter Sellers in *The Prisoner of Zenda* (1979) as look-alikes

Mel Brooks in *The History of the World, Part I* (1981) as King Louis and his look-alike Jacques the Pissboy

Mark Lester in *Crossed Swords* (1978), a remake of *The Prince and the Pauper*

Lee Marvin as Kid Shelleen in *Cat Ballou* (1965), as well as Tim Strawn, his killer brother with a silver nose—the real one having been bitten off in a fight

Yul Brynner as American and communist spies in *The Double Man* (1967)

Hayley Mills in *The Parent Trap* (1961) as twin sisters

Charles Gray as a whole bunch of nefarious Blofelds in *Diamonds Are Forever* (1971)

Boris Karloff as good/evil twins in *The Black Room* (1935)

Brigitte Helm in *Metropolis* (1926), as a proponent for rights of the downtrodden, and as the robot-double created to undermine her efforts

Barbara Steele as Princesses Asa and Katia in *Black Sunday* (1960) who, though separated by centuries, are dead ringers

Katharine Ross also got to play a human and her robot dupe in *The Stepford Wives* (1975)

Raymond Massey in *Things to Come* (1936), as John Cabal and his grandson Oswald

IT'S A DRAG

Leading men who have dressed as women on the screen:

Adam West in *The Happy Hooker Goes to Hollywood* (1979)

Tony Curtis in *Some Like It Hot* (1959)

Yul Brynner in *The Magic Christian* (1970)

Lon Chaney, Sr., in *The Unholy Three* (1930)

Burt Lancaster in *The Crimson Pirate* (1952)

Lionel Barrymore in *The Devil Doll* (1936)

Michel Serrault in *La Cage aux Folles* (1979)

Michael Caine in *Dressed to Kill* (1980)

Peter Sellers in *The Mouse That Roared* (1959)

Arthur Lucan in the "Mother Riley" series, including *Old Mother Riley Meets the Vampire* (1952)

Lou Costello in *Lost in a Harem* (1944)

Jerry Lewis in *At War With the Army* (1950)

Cary Grant in *I Was a Male War Bride* (1949)

Alec Guinness in *Kind Hearts and Coronets* (1949)

Stan Laurel in *Jitterbugs* (1943)

Jack Benny in *Charley's Aunt* (1941)

Bob Hope in *The Princess and the Pirate* (1944)

Lee J. Cobb in *In Like Flint* (1967)

George Sanders in *The Kremlin Letter* (1970)

Dudley Moore in *Bedazzled* (1967)

Joe E. Brown in *Shut My Big Mouth* (1942)

Jack Gilford in *A Funny Thing Happened on the Way to the Forum* (1966)

BACK TO FRONT

Courtesy of *The Second Signet Book of Movie Lists*, a movie trivia game to be played for amusement and enlightenment. Simply pick a film title, and have your opponent name a film that begins with the *last* word of the title you've selected. You must then do the same with your adversary's title. For example, a game might evolve like this, with "The" and "A" discounted, and compound words acceptable:

Now You See Him, Now You Don't (1972)
Don't Fence Me In (1945)
In the Heat of the Night (1967)
Night of the Living Dead (1968)
Dead Run (1969)
Run Silent, Run Deep (1958)
Deep in My Heart (1954)
Heartbreak Kid (1972)
Kid from Texas (1950)
Texas Across the River (1966)
River of No Return (1954)
Return of Dr. X (1939)
X the Unknown (1956)
Unknown Terror (1957)
Terror Is a Man (1959)
Man With a Million (1954)
Million Dollar Baby (1941)
Baby, the Rain Must Fall (1965)
Fall of the Roman Empire (1964)
Empire of the Ants (1977)

The trick is to keep the game *going*. Obviously, it could have otherwise ended with *Heartbreak Kid*, to which the response would be *Kid Galahad* and the end of the game. You lose if your opponent flubs it and you *haven't* got a film to fill the bill. This is also an interesting game for solitary players. (Incidentally, one-word titles like *The Deep* count. It matters if you're trying to break a listing record or toss a word back into your foe's court.)

WHO WAS THAT MASKED MAN?

Unusual disguises in the movies, for purposes of infiltration, spying, or casing:

Gene Hackman dressed as Santa Claus in *The French Connection* (1971)

Cleavon Little disguised as a Ku Klux Klan member in *Blazing Saddles* (1974)

Roy Kinnear costumed as a bear in *The Three Musketeers* (1974)

Donald Sutherland, painted green and poked into a coffin as a corpse in *The Great Train Robbery* (1979)

Woody Allen as a robot butler in *Sleeper* (1973)

Lou Costello trying to pass as Dracula in *Abbott and Costello Meet Frankenstein* (1948)

An anonymous extra disguised as a tomato to infiltrate the army of monster fruits in *Attack of the Killer Tomatoes* (1978). (He gives himself away when, sitting around the campfire, having dinner, he asks one of the tomatoes to pass the catsup—an incongruous act of cannibalism!)

HAPPY BIRTHDAY TO YOU!

Actors who age significantly in the course of a motion picture:

Edward Judd in *First Men in the Moon* (1965), some thirty years old at the beginning of the film and nearly ninety by the end.

Dustin Hoffman in *Little Big Man* (1970), as Jack Crabb, a 121-year-old former pioneer, who reminisces about the Old West.

Keir Dullea in *2001: A Space Odyssey* (1968), as an astronaut who goes from youth to senility in an elaborate "cage" on an alien world.

Barbra Streisand in *Funny Lady* (1975), growing from young lady to matron as Fanny Brice.

Christopher Lee in *Horror of Dracula* (1958), wherein, rather than aging normally, the vampire's many centuries catch up with him in an instant, reducing him to dust.

Charlton Heston in *The Ten Commandments* (1956), from the baby in the bulrush to a white-bearded old prophet.

Orson Welles in *Citizen Kane* (1940), seen as a suddenly wealthy child and as a friendless, expiring old man.

Nigel Terry in *Excalibur* (1981), a film which follows King Arthur from the moment of conception to his death decades later.

Claude Heater in *Ben-Hur* (1959), one of many biblical epics in which Jesus is seen from the time he's a babe until his crucifixion.

Laurence Olivier in *Wuthering Heights* (1939), seen as a

young Heathcliff, a rough little boy; and as a gray, emaciated Heathcliff who dies in search of his lost love.

Burt Lancaster in *Birdman of Alcatraz* (1962), as convict Robert Stroud, in which forty-three years of the prisoner's life are detailed, sixty-four years in all.

James Cagney in *Yankee Doodle Dandy* (1942), as George Michael Cohan, from boyhood to retirement.

Ursula Andress in *She* (1965), who holds a record: 2,000 years in a few moments.

Katharine Hepburn in *Song of Love* (1947), as Clara Schumann, wife of composer Robert, from wedding to widowhood.

Sophia Loren in *Lady L* (1966), from the age of eighteen to eighty.

Tyrone Power in *The Long Gray Line* (1955), as a youth-to-retirement West Pointer named Marty Maher.

WINNER TAKES ALL

The finest one-on-one races, fights, contests, and the like in film history:

Rocky (1976): The climactic boxing championship between Rocky Balboa (Sylvester Stallone) and Apollo Creed (Carl Weathers).

Ben-Hur (1959): The chariot race, which, though it took place in a crowded field, was really between Judah Ben-Hur (Charlton Heston) and Messala (Stephen Boyd).

The Adventures of Robin Hood (1938): The rousing duel between Robin (Errol Flynn) and the wicked Sir Guy of Gisbourne (Basil Rathbone).

Raiders of the Lost Ark (1981): Indiana Jones (Harrison Ford) battles a Nazi for the truck they both want—the one gripping sequence in an otherwise fast but dumb picture.

2001: A Space Odyssey (1968): Astronaut Bowman (Keir Dullea) vs. the lunatic computer HAL, when the latter refuses to let the spaceman back into his vessel.

King Kong (1933): The original—giant ape battles a tyrannosaur for ownership of Ann Darrow (Fay Wray).

Jaws (1975): Sheriff Brody (Roy Scheider) gunning for the Great White Shark in the closing moments of the film.

The Exorcist (1973): The knockdown purging of Regan (Linda Blair) by Father Karras (Jason Miller).

Tarzan's Greatest Adventure (1959): A little-known but humdinger battle between the Ape Man (Gordon Scott) and the villainous Slade (Anthony Quayle).

Their struggle takes place atop a cliff, with Tarzan empty-handed, Slade wielding a long-stemmed garrote.

North by Northwest (1959): Roger Thornhill (Cary Grant) being chased by a crop-duster in an open field, and luring it into a spectacular crack-up.

Moby Dick (1956): Though less spectacular than the novel, the final conflict between the white whale and Captain Ahab (Gregory Peck) is one of the greatest of all time.

The Seventh Voyage of Sinbad (1958): Sinbad (Kerwin Mathews) engages a living skeleton in a swordfight, one of the most startling fantasy sequences in all of cinema.

El Cid (1962): The joust between Rodrigo Diaz de Bivar (Charlton Heston) and Don Martin (Christopher Rhodes) for possession of Calahorra, a disputed city.

NAME ABOVE THE TITLE

Writers or filmmakers whose names are actually *part* of their films' titles:

Jacqueline Susann's Once Is Not Enough (1975)
Fellini's Casanova (1977)
Russ Meyers' Vixens (197)
Gore Vidal's Caligula (1979) (Vidal's name was removed before film opened.)
Agatha Christie's The Mirror Crack'd (1980)
Cheech and Chong's Nice Dreams (1981)
Abbott and Costello Meet Frankenstein (1948) (and the entire series of Abbott and Costello films)
Hemingway's Adventures of a Young Man (1962)
Jules Verne's Rocket to the Moon (1967)
Neil Simon's I Ought to Be in Pictures (1982)
Andy Warhol's Frankenstein (1974)

A HERO IS MORE THAN A SANDWICH

The screen's most stirring moments of heroism:

Birth of a Nation (1915): Confederate soldier Ben Cameron (Henry B. Walthall) ramming his flag down the mouth of a Union cannon.

The Dawn Patrol (1938): Captain Courtney (Errol Flynn), piloting a biplane, sneaking into enemy territory to bomb an ammunition dump. As if the mission were not enough, he must simultaneously battle the German ace Von Richter—who slays the heroic Englishman.

Gunga Din (1939): Sam Jaffe, as the legendary waterboy, climbs to the top of a temple to bugle his comrades, warning the British troops that they are riding into a trap.

The Alamo (1960): Call it pure hokum, the death of Davy Crockett (John Wayne), run through with pokers and otherwise wounded, heaving a torch into the ammo dump, is heroic magic.

The Magnificent Seven (1960): Long before the climactic gun battle, Chris (Yul Brynner) and Vin (Steve McQueen) agree to drive a hearse to the cemetery—against the wishes of the townfolk. They make it, Vin riding shotgun and Chris guiding the horses with sheer brass.

Bridge on the River Kwai (1957): Shears (William Holden), shot and dying, dragging himself from the river to prevent Col. Nicholson (Alec Guinness) from disconnecting the explosives affixed to the bridge.

The Flame and the Arrow (1950): Dardo (Burt Lancaster) fighting off four well-armed soldiers using only a torch—one of the many superheroic scenes in this film.

A HERO IS MORE THAN A SANDWICH (continued)

El Cid (1962): Rodrigo Diaz de Bivar (Charlton Heston) rescuing an abducted prince by battling thirteen knights single-handedly.

High Noon (1952): Will Kane (Gary Cooper) in his immortal lone stand against a quartet of gunslingers.

Mighty Joe Young (1949): The giant gorilla rescuing a baby from the top of a burning orphanage.

ACTING ACTORS

Actors who starred in films about other actors:

James Cagney as Lon Chaney, Sr., in *Man of a Thousand Faces* (1957)

Julie Andrews as Gertrude Lawrence in *Star* (1968)

Carroll Baker as Jean Harlow in *Harlow* (1965)

Carol Lynley as Jean Harlow in *Harlow* (1965)

Dorothy Malone as Diana Barrymore, Errol Flynn as John Barrymore in *Too Much, Too Soon* (1958); Jack Cassidy was Barrymore in *W.C. Fields and Me* (1976)

Ray Danton as George Raft in *The George Raft Story* (1961)

Donald O'Connor as Buster Keaton in *The Buster Keaton Story* (1957)

Will Rogers, Jr., as his father in *The Story of Will Rogers* (1952)

Anthony Dexter as *Valentino* (1951)

Rudolf Nureyev as *Valentino* (1979)

Larry Parks as Al Jolson in *The Jolson Story* (1946)

James Brolin and Jill Clayburgh as *Gable and Lombard* (1976)

Rod Steiger in the starring role of *W.C. Fields and Me* (1976)

Glenda Jackson as Sarah Bernhardt in *The Incredible Sarah* (1976)

HEROD ANTIPAS ON FILM

In the first volume, we offered up the films' Pontius Pilates. Herewith, his partner in death:

Charles Laughton in *Salome* (1953)

Herbert Lom in *The Big Fisherman* (1959)

Frank Thring in *King of Kings* (1961) (Thring was Pilate in *Ben-Hur* two years before)

Francesco Leonetti in *The Gospel According to St. Matthew* (1964)

José Ferrer in *The Greatest Story Ever Told* (1965)

Joshua Mostel (son of Zero) in *Jesus Christ Superstar* (1973)

X MARKS THE SPOT

"X" is also unique in that fewer films have used it in their title than any other letter. Herewith, a list of every picture beginning with the tough little letter:

X-15 (1961)
X, the Man With the X-Ray Eyes (1963)
X the Unknown (1956)
X, Y, and Zee (1972)
Xanadu (1980)

For the record, the usually difficult "Z" and "Q" have twenty-four and thirty films to their credit.

ROMANS À CLEF

Movies that pretended to have nothing to do with the real-life subject matter on which they were based:

Citizen Kane (1940): Orson Welles has long claimed that this is not the story of publishing magnate and citizen of the world William Randolph Hearst. If Mr. Welles is right, he's the only one who thinks so.

Where Love Has Gone (1964): Based on the Harold Robbins novel which was based on the sensational Johnny Stompanato murder. Bette Davis plays Lana Turner, Joey Heatherton her daughter Cheryl . . . if you believe in art imitating life.

The Wild Party (1975): James Coco as Fatty Arbuckle.

All That Jazz (1980): Unlike Orson Welles, director Bob Fosse will admit that the film was *inspired* by his life—but that's where the similarity ends. The fact that both Fosse and his character Joe Gideon (Roy Scheider) could be clones from their careers—choreographer/film director—to their love affairs to their heart attack to their friendship with Ben Vereen makes any deeper association obviously unfounded.

The Bad and the Beautiful (1952): In general, a fictitious account of the rise and fall of a Hollywood mogul—though the character of Jonathan Shields (Kirk Douglas) is clearly drawn from the late Val Lewton. Indeed, in an overt "homage" to Lewton, whose big initial hit was *The Cat People* (1943), Shields' first smash is *Son of the Cat People*.

The Godfather (1972): While Don Corleone is a pastiche figure, the character of his godson Johnny, a singer who desperately wants to star in an upcoming motion picture, is patterned after Frank Sinatra and his quest for a part in *From Here to Eternity*.

The Arrangement (1969): Elia Kazan's semiautobiographical bestseller was the basis for this film starring Kirk Douglas. Though Eddie Anderson (Douglas) is an advertising executive to Kazan's author/director in real life, the impact of success and its alienation are straight from Kazan's own world.

SPECTACLES

Movies where the focus of an important scene, or the outcome of the story itself, was influenced by a pair of glasses:

Superman II (1981): When Lois Lane innocently yanks off Clark Kent's glasses to clean them, she first notices the resemblance between Clark and Superman. This leads to her discovering his secret identity, the Man of Steel giving up his powers to make love to her, and the world nearly falling in the interim before the might of supervillains from Superman's native world of Krypton.

Time After Time (1979): H. G. Wells (Malcolm McDowell) uses his time machine to travel from the turn of the century to the present in pursuit of Jack the Ripper. As his glasses are damaged, he sneaks into a display of Wellsabilia in order to steal a pair of his old lenses.

Dr. Cyclops (1940): Albert Dekker is the sinister scientist who shrinks people. He perishes when, having lost his glasses, he tumbles down a well. The title of the film euphemistically describes his blindness.

X, the Man with the X-Ray Eyes (1963): The remarkable scientist is unable to control his penetrating vision, and can see "normally" only if he keeps his eyes shut and wears thick sunglasses.

Tarzan's Greatest Adventure (1959): The Jungle Lord would never have had to battle the evil Slade (Anthony Quayle) for his life, if Slade hadn't booted his partner into a pit when the latter was groping about for his glasses. All the partner wanted was to get wealthy and run.

SPECTACLES (continued)

Plus some noted glasses-wearers:

Benjamin Franklin (Howard da Silva) in *1776* (1972)
Hooper (Richard Dreyfuss) in *Jaws* (1975)

AU NATUREL

Foreign films widely shown in the United States without a title change or translation:

La Cage aux Folles (1979)
La Cage aux Folles II (1981)
La Dolce Vita (1961)
La Strada (1954)
Fellini Roma (1972)
Sallah (1964)
Kwaidan (1965)
L'Invitation (1973)
Lacombe, Lucien (1974)
Dersu Uzala (1975)
Madame Rosa (1977)
Cousin, Cousine (1976)

A DINKY BY ANY OTHER NAME

Some curious names used as titles of motion pictures:

Dinky (1935) with li'l Jackie Cooper
Fluffy (1965), a lion
Dimples (1936) with Shirley Temple
Digy (1974), a dog
Duffy (1968), a crime caper
Dulcy (1940), an orphan
Dondi (1961), a comic strip
Mothra (1962), a giant moth
Nabonga (1944), a gorilla
Mogambo (1953), Clark Gable in Africa
Huk (1956), a vengeance flick
Hud (1963) with Paul Newman
Samar (1962), a prison flick

BUNCHA BEASTS

Movies with animals in their titles:

The Spider (1957)
Empire of the Ants (1977)
Zebra in the Kitchen (1965)
A Tiger Walks (1964)
The Lion (1962)
Namu the Killer Whale (1966)
Day of the Dolphin (1973)
The Day the Fish Came Out (1967)
Lord of the Flies (1963)
The Deadly Mantis (1957)
Tarantula (1955)
Horse Feathers (1932)
Duck Soup (1933)
The Alligator People (1959)
The Fly (1958)
The Deadly Bees (1967)
Monkey Business (1952)
A Boy and His Dog (1975)
The Day of the Jackal (1973)
The Day of the Locust (1975)
Hugo the Hippo (1976)
The Bashful Elephant (1962)

QUADRUPLE-DIGIT MOVIES

Motion pictures with rather large numbers in their titles:

The Phantom from Ten Thousand Leagues (1955)
The 5,000 Fingers of Dr. T (1953)
Twenty Thousand Leagues Under the Sea (1954)
80,000 Suspects (1963)
The Beast from 20,000 Fathoms (1953)
Five Million Years to Earth (1968)
Twenty Million Miles to Earth (1957)
One Million Years, B.C. (1966)
One Million B.C. (1940)
The Beast with a Million Eyes (1955)
How to Steal a Million (1966)
Man with a Million (1954)
Billion Dollar Brain (1967)
1001 Arabian Nights (1959)
Twenty Million Sweethearts (1934)
Ten Thousand Bedrooms (1957)

TITLE TIME

No, not the date for a heavyweight bout—but motion pictures with times of the day in their titles:

Twelve O'Clock High (1949)
High Noon (1952)
Five Miles to Midnight (1963)
3:10 to Yuma (1957)
Eight O'Clock Walk (1952)
Bomb at 10:10 (1966)

. . . and some general chronometric increments:

Thirty Seconds Over Tokyo (1944)
Nine Hours to Rama (1963)
The Seven Minutes (1971)
One Day in the Life of Ivan Denisovitch (1971)
Five Weeks in a Balloon (1962)
Thirty Years of Fun (1963)

SHOWOFF!

The most amazing feats of strength ever seen in the movies:

Superman (1978): The Man of Steel diving inside the earth and pushing together the rending seams of the San Andreas Fault.

Hercules (1957): Steve Reeves as the son of Zeus, raising a huge tree trunk above his head and hurling it in the path of a runaway chariot. ·

Samson and Delilah (1949): The blinded Samson pulling down the temple of the fish-god Dagon.

Quo Vadis (1951): The mighty servant Ursus (Buddy Baer) rescuing the bound Ligia (Deborah Kerr) from a wild bull by breaking the animal's neck.

Popeye (1980): The squint-eyed sailor (Robin Williams) decking "The Dirtiest Fighter Alive," one Oxblood Oxheart, with his famous "twisker" punch.

The Spy Who Loved Me (1977): The extraordinary "Jaws" (Richard Kiel), finding himself in a tank with a giant shark, tearing the man-eater to pieces.

The World's Greatest Athlete (1973): The jungle-bred Nanu (Jan-Michael Vincent) attending Merrivale College and, in turn, shattering the NCAA records for the pole vault, high jump, long jump, javelin throw, shot put, and discus throw.

Flash Gordon (1936): Flash (Buster Crabbe), a captive on the alien world of Mongo, must battle a succession of monsters in the Tournament of Death. Each, including a horned gorilla, is infinitely more powerful than he, but Flash triumphs.

Tarzan Goes to India (1962): The Ape Man (Jock Ma-

SHOWOFF! (continued)

honey) is lashed between a pair of oxen, whose goal is
to tear him in twain. He manages to restrain them.

Doc Savage (1975): Ron Ely as the Man of Bronze turning and punching an oncoming assailant. The blow is
so powerful that the man flies backward across the
room and duckpins into fellow thugs.

ANOTHER PUZZLER

If the challenge of *Back to Front* was not a fit test of your cinematic knowledge, here's another little game: take a motion picture name and, using the last letters of the first and surname, come up with another name. For example:

Bette Davis (actress)
Everett Sloane (actor)
Tom Ewell (actor)
Mervyn LeRoy (director)
Ned Young (screenwriter)
David (Wark) Griffith (director)
Dustin Hoffman (actor)
Nick Nolte (actor)

. . . and so on. Once again, don't fling a name at your opponent unless *you* have a response to ward off a challenge. Reference books are permitted only if your answer is challenged.

USELESS

In our first volume of movie lists, we cited the best and worst film books ever written. This time out, we present a collection of the film titles which have the most limited appeal of any in the field. Why they were published, save for a tax write-off, is an unfathomable mystery:

Focus on Shoot the Piano Player by Leo Braudy, Prentice-Hall, 1972

True, the 1962 François Truffaut film is a gem. But who really cares about the Anarchist Imagination of the director?

Screenwriter: The Life and Times of Nunnally Johnson by Tom Stempel, A. S. Barnes, 1980

A great screenwriter, witness *The Grapes of Wrath* and *The Three Faces of Eve*. But Mr. Stempel, Associate Professor of Cinema at Los Angeles City College, is unlikely to sell many copies except to his students.

Film in Sweden: The New Directors by Stig Björkman, A. S. Barnes, 1977

Only for those interested in Lasse Forsberg and Bo Widerberg.

Zombie, the Living Dead by Rose London, Bounty Books, 1976

A rather specialized subject, unless you were wondering about the ad copy for *The Thing that Couldn't Die* ("They chopped off its head and buried it for 400 years . . . yet it lives today!")

The Supernatural Movie Quizbook by Jeff Rovin, Drake, 1977

The most insignificant compendium of worthless trivia in the history of publishing. Bar none.

USING THEIR HEAD

Some unlikely objects used by special effects technicians to represent the Real McCoy:

Clash of the Titans (1981): The blood of the beheaded Medusa was, in fact, wallpaper paste dyed red.

The Giant Behemoth (1959): An exploding oil tank was actually several film cans stacked one atop the other.

Close Encounters of the Third Kind (1977): The swirling clouds concealing the massive mother ship were not vapor but white paint filmed as it was injected into water.

The Good Earth (1937): The swarm of locusts blighting the land, angry hordes of coffee grounds poured into water.

The Beginning or the End (1947): To duplicate an atom blast in this story of the Manhattan Project, the special-effects team poured powder into a tank, the powder bottoming out and looking like an inverse blast. Since the camera was positioned upside-down, the effect was quite realistic.

2001: A Space Odyssey (1968): The massive spaceship *Discovery* was actually constructed from thousands of bits and pieces cannibalized from plastic hobby kits. This technique was also used to build the spaceships in *Star Wars.*

Superman (1978): Why leave Christopher Reeve hanging around on wires for the long shots? Wherever possible, the flying Superman was actually a radio-controlled doll, some eighteen inches long, flying along an invisible wire.

INITIAL REACTION

Movies with initials in the title:

B.F.'s Daughter (1948)
B.S. I Love You (1971)
C.C. and Co. (1970)
The D.I. (1957)
D.O.A. (1949)
The F.B.I. Story (1959)
FM (1978)
G.I. Blues (1960)
H.M. Pulham, Esq. (1941)
I.F. Stone's Weekly (1973)
J.D.'s Revenge (1976)
J.W. Coop (1972)
The Liberation of L.B. Jones (1970)
Mackintosh and T.J. (1975)
O.S.S. (1946)
P.J. (1968)
R.P.M. (1970)
S.O.S. Pacific (1960)
S.O.S. Coastguard (1937)
T.R. Baskin (1970)
UFO (1956)
The V.I.P.s (1963)
W.C. Fields and Me (1976)
W.W. and the Dixie Dancekings (1975)
WAC from Walla Walla (1952)
Welcome to L.A. (1977)
WUSA (1970)
Z.P.G. (1972)

A SPOT OF HUMOR

Here's the last puzzler you'll get in this volume of Movie Lists: create an unlikely (and telling) double bill which will stand out on a marquee! Some examples:

When Strangers Marry, You Belong to Me
I Wake Up Screaming, In the Heat of the Night
The Lady Vanishes, Twenty Thousand Leagues Under the Sea
King Kong vs. Godzilla, Bob & Carol & Ted & Alice
The Importance of Being Earnest, Islands in the Stream
Planet of the Apes, Monkey Business
The Titanic, Don't Drink the Water
The Diamond Queen, La Cage aux Folles
How to Murder Your Wife, Diary of a Bachelor
Crime and Punishment, . . . And Justice for All
Young Winston, A Chump at Oxford
Cast a Giant Shadow, The Day the Earth Caught Fire
Exodus, The Birth of a Nation
Intolerance, Divorce American Style
Baby the Rain Must Fall, Deluge
The Invisible Man, Now You See Him, Now You Don't
Cold Turkey, A Lion in Winter
The Towering Inferno, Man on Fire
The Greatest Show on Earth, Star Trek
Rodan, Thirty Seconds Over Tokyo
Rollerball, Winning

Actors and actresses who have donned eye makeup to pass for Orientals:

Warner Oland: *Charlie Chan Carries On* (1931) and its many sequels

Boris Karloff: *The Mask of Fu Manchu* (1932)

Paul Muni: *The Good Earth* (1937)

Lana Turner: *The Adventures of Marco Polo* (1938)

Sidney Toler: *Charlie Chan at Treasure Island* (1939) and sequels

Katharine Hepburn: *Dragon Seed* (1944)

Rex Harrison: *Anna and the King of Siam* (1946)

John Wayne: *The Conqueror* (1955) (as Genghis Khan)

Yul Brynner: *The King and I* (1956)

Marlon Brando: *The Teahouse of the August Moon* (1956)

Flora Robson: *55 Days at Peking* (1963)

Christopher Lee: *The Face of Fu Manchu* (1965)

Stephen Boyd: *Genghis Khan* (1965)

Anthony Quinn: *Marco the Magnificent* (1966) (as Kublai Khan)

Sean Connery: *You Only Live Twice* (1967)

Peter Lorre: *Think Fast, Mr. Moto* (1937) and the seven films which followed

John Emery: *Blood on the Sun* (1945) as Premier Tanaka

Helen Hayes in *The Son-Daughter* (1932)

Jennifer Jones in *Love Is a Many Splendored Thing* (1955)

Mickey Rooney in *Breakfast at Tiffany's* (1961)

George Raft in *Limehouse Blues* (1934)

Alec Guinness in *A Majority of One* (1961)

PARTING SHOTS

Asked to offer their own one-line self-appraisals, these stars said this of themselves:

"He did his job and kept his promises," Charlton Heston

"He was ugly, was strong, and had dignity," John Wayne

"He was lucky and he knew it," Clark Gable

"I was just a guy gifted with good looks I had done nothing to earn," Robert Taylor

"I'm a personality as well as an actress," Katharine Hepburn

"The only achievement I am really proud of is the friends I have made in this community (Hollywood)," Gary Cooper

"I'm the guy who always squawks about roles, but never refuses to play one," Humphrey Bogart

"Acting is not the beginning and the end of everything," James Cagney

"I don't want to be profound or intellectual," Kirk Douglas

"Naturally restless, I frequently find myself rebelling inwardly at the deadly routine of picture-making," Errol Flynn

"He fought being typecast," Burt Lancaster

"Why relegate me to playing Mexican bandits and redskins? Why can I not play a pope, or an Eskimo, an Indian, a Greek, an Italian?" Anthony Quinn

"I don't always like myself as I am, and if I hadn't been able to become an actor I'd have been in despair," Laurence Olivier

"Here lies Elizabeth Taylor. Thank you for every moment, good and bad. I've enjoyed it all," Elizabeth Taylor

PARTING SHOTS (continued)

"I don't like anything about acting. But I did very well by it," Spencer Tracy

"He tried not to be a shmuck, and occasionally he succeeded," Gene Wilder

"He didn't give a damn about how a character's mind worked. All he cared about was getting to the studio on time and remembering his lines," Omar Sharif

IT'S A TOUGH LIFE

You've got to admire anyone who can make a living in the movies. The old bromide about there being 36,000 members of the Screen Actors Guild with only 2,000 of those earning above poverty level is absolutely true. Only a handful of those 2,000 are in the megabuck category. Even the well-known names have to compromise, however, as fads and fortunes change. Here are stars who have appeared in some of the finest and most popular films of all time—and who have been forced to accept less just to earn a living.

Louis Jourdan, the charismatic star of *Gigi* (1958), a film which won nine Academy Awards, was most recently seen in *Swamp Thing*, a horror film based on a rather silly comic book.

Orson Welles, the boy genius who made *Citizen Kane* (1940), hasn't made a picture in years and is selling wine on TV.

Victor Mature, the popular 1950s he-man and star of *Samson and Delilah* (1949), was last seen on the screen in *Head* (1968), a near-invisible motion picture starring the TV rock group The Monkees.

Joan Crawford, a class-act Oscar winner, who made a graceful transition to high-grade horror films with *What Ever Happened to Baby Jane?* (1962), stayed with the genre too long. One of her last films was *Trog* (1970), in which she found herself bringing a caveman back to life. . . .

Lana Turner, like Crawford, ultimately went into horror films. Hers, unfortunately, was an aborted effort with the low-budget, low-quality, low-mentality *Persecution*

(1974). Oh, for the days of *The Postman Always Rings Twice* (1946) and *The Bad and the Beautiful* (1952).

Ava Gardner, one of the great stars in the history of cinema, was last seen on the screen as Lorne Greene's *daughter* in *Earthquake* (1974), one of many actors seen all too briefly in that star-laden disaster epic.

James Stewart, a legend in his own time, was last seen doing a floppo TV series. He has not acted since.

ROWDY REMAKES

Adult and pornographic remakes, sequels, interpretations, etc., of famous motion pictures:

Sex World: takes you where *Westworld* and *Futureworld* leave off.

Tarzoon, Shame of the Jungle: the real story of the Jungle Lord.

Flesh Gordon: off to the planet Porno for the one-time ice-cream hero.

The Sexorcist: devilish doings, in more ways than one.

Cream Rinse: billed as "an erotic sequel to *Shampoo*."

Ms. Magnificent: originally entitled *Superwoman*, changed by court order. As the ads claimed, "She does two things extremely well. One of them is fly."

M*A*S*H'd: the title says it all.

All the Senator's Girls: what Woodward and Bernstein didn't discover.

2069: A Sex Odyssey: HAL would turn in his deep-space grave.

Carnal Encounters of the Barest Kind: "We Do Not Sleep Alone!"

Rollerbabies: *Rollerball* was a substitute for war. . . .

THE BOND WOMEN

The ladies who played opposite James Bond in his many
adventures . . . and the actresses who brought them to
life:

1. Honeychile Rider (Ursula Andress) in *Dr. No*
2. Tatiana Romanova (Daniela Bianchi) in *From Russia With Love*
3. Pussy Galore (Honor Blackman) in *Goldfinger*
4. Domino (Claudine Auger) in *Thunderball*
5. Kissy Sazuki (Mie Hama) in *You Only Live Twice*
6. Tracy Vicenzo (Diana Rigg) in *On Her Majesty's Secret Service*
7. Tiffany Case (Jill St. John) in *Diamonds Are Forever*
8. Solitaire (Jane Seymour) in *Live and Let Die*
9. Mary Goodnight (Britt Ekland) in *The Man With the Golden Gun*
10. Major Anya Asamova (Barbara Bach) in *The Spy Who Loved Me*
11. Holly Goodhead (Lois Chiles) in *Moonraker*
12. Melina Havelock (Carole Bouquet) in *For Your Eyes Only*

Charlton Heston as Andrew Jackson in *The Buccaneer*. Disguised
beside him—he's wearing hair—is Yul Brynner as the pirate-patriot
Jean Lafitte. See *REAGAN'S FOREBEARS*, page 3.

An extremely rare still from *Dreams of the Rarebit Fiend*. See
IS THIS ANY WAY TO RUN AN AIRLINE?, page 111.

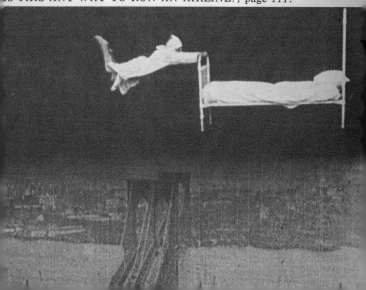

The 125-story-tall skyscaper goes down in flames in *The Tower ing Inferno*. See *AUTHOR! AUTHOR!*, page *17*.

The big top burns in *Circus World*. See *YOU'RE FIRED!*, page *23*.

Robert Ryan in *Captain Nemo and the Underwater City*. See *ALL ASHORE*, page 137.

Sally Field as *The Flying Nun*. See *MULTIMEDIA MIRACLES*, page *24*.

The plum-color outfitted *Zorro, the Gay Blade*, starring George Hamilton. See *WHIPPED!!*, page *44*.

Neil McCarthy as the satyr Calibos in *Clash of the Titans*. See *HATE-LOVE*, page *145*.

François Truffaut and director Steven Spielberg (in hat) discuss a scene for *Close Encounters of the Third Kind*. See *ACTING DIRECTORS*, page 40

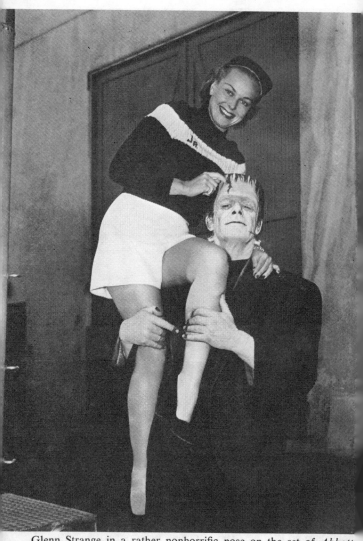

Glenn Strange in a rather nonhorrific pose on the set of *Abbott and Costello Meet Frankenstein*. See *SUPERMEN*, page *100*.

Peter O'Toole as Cervantes impersonating Don Quixote in *Man of La Mancha*. See *CAN'T STOP AT ONE*, page *123*.

Director Robert Wise and George C. Scott examine the miniature model of *The Hindenburg* used in that film. See *CATASTRO-PHE!* page *98*.

Lily Tomlin, as the pint-sized Pat Kramer, is menaced by a toy robot in *The Incredible Shrinking Woman*. See *SEX CHANGE*, page 110.

Another landmark bites the dust.—from *Gorgo*. See *LANDMARK ACTION*, page *92*.

Farrah Fawcett, Burt Reynolds, Roger Moore, and Dean Martin in *The Cannonball Run*. See *COMEBACKS!*, page *12*.

Gene Wilder, seen here as the Fox in *The Little Prince*. See
PARTING SHOTS, page *81.*

Karen Black and friend, stewardesses who are about to try and fly a crippled 747 in *Airport 1975*. See *HATE-LOVE*, page *145*.
© UNIVERSAL PICTURES

Andre Teuber and Richard Burton in *Doctor Faustus*. See *THE DEVIL, YOU SAY!*, page 99.

Trevor Howard and Marlon Brando in *Mutiny on the Bounty*, before setting sail on their fateful voyage. See *STACKING UP*, page 103.

A rare, unusual still of the young Walt Disney. See *UNCA WALT*, page *148*.
© WALT DISNEY PRODUCTIONS

Will Penny, starring Charlton Heston as a cowboy nearing the half-century mark. See *LOVE-HATE*, page *143*.

URBAN BLIGHT

Cities which have been razed in science-fiction films:

1. San Francisco, by a giant octopus in *It Came from Beneath the Sea* (1955)
2. London by *Gorgo* (1961)
3. Tokyo by *Godzilla* (1954)
4. Las Vegas by *The Amazing Colossal Man* (1957)
5. Washington, D.C., by aliens in *Earth vs. the Flying Saucers* (1956)
6. Los Angeles in *War of the Colossal Beast* (1958)
7. Copenhagen by *Reptilicus* (1962)
8. Rome in *Twenty Million Miles to Earth* (1957)
9. San Diego in *Attack of the Killer Tomatoes* (1978)
10. New York in *The Beast from Twenty Thousand Fathoms* (1953)

STARS IN THE STARS

Popular, mainstream actors who have gone into outer space in movies, or played aliens:

Jerry Lewis in *Way, Way Out* (1966)
Charlton Heston in *Planet of the Apes* (1968)
Kirk Douglas in *Saturn III* (1980)
Sean Connery in *Outland* (1981)
Alec Guinness in *Star Wars* (1977)
Max von Sydow in *Flash Gordon* (1980)
Marlon Brando in *Superman* (1978)
Maximilian Schell in *The Black Hole* (1979)
Jane Fonda in *Barbarella* (1968)
Richard Dreyfuss in *Close Encounters of the Third Kind* (1977)
Claude Rains in *Battle of the Worlds* (1960)
Christopher Plummer in *Starcrash* (1978)

DOMETOPS

The most famous bald-headed characters in motion pictures:

The King and I (1956): Yul Brynner as the King of Siam

Superman (1978): Gene Hackman as the hairless Lex Luthor

Dr. Cyclops (1940): Albert Dekker as the bald scientist

Star Trek (1979): Persis Khambatta as Ilia, the hairless Deltan

The Amazing Colossal Man (1957): Glenn Langan is permanently depilated by a plutonium bomb blast

Mad Love (1935): Peter Lorre as the crazed—and hairless—Dr. Gogol

Flash Gordon (1980): Max von Sydow as the bald Emperor Ming of Mongo

Tower of London (1939): Boris Karloff as the skin-headed torturer-executioner Mord

Annie (1982): Albert Finney as Daddy Warbucks in this $30,000,000 musical

The Thing (1951): James Arness as the outer-space carrotman

The Seventh Seal (1956): Bengt Ekerot as Death

Apocalypse Now (1979): Marlon Brando as the lunatic officer

LONG LIVE THE KING

Although *Excalibur* was one of the most popular films of 1981, it was far from the first time the saga of King Arthur has been brought to the screen. Actors who have played the role of the legendary leader in films are:

William Farnum in *A Connecticut Yankee* (1931)

Sir Cedric Hardwicke in *A Connecticut Yankee in King Arthur's Court* (1949)

Brian Aherne in *Prince Valiant* (1954)

Mel Ferrer in *Knights of the Round Table* (1954)

Anthony Bushell in *The Black Knight* (1954)

Mark Dignam in *Siege of the Saxons* (1963)

Rickie Sorensen (voice) in *The Sword and the Stone* (1963), a cartoon feature from Walt Disney Productions

Richard Harris in *Camelot* (1967)

Graham Chapman in *Monty Python and the Holy Grail* (1975) (Chapman played other parts in the film as well.)

Kenneth More in *Unidentified Flying Oddball* (1979)

Nigel Terry in *Excalibur* (1981)

OH, TO BE YOUNG AGAIN!

Though most great men and women are more fascinating in their sage later years, motion pictures prefer their vital youths. Hence, the following:

Young Bess (1953), the story of the legendary Queen Elizabeth

Young Daniel Boone (1950), even younger than Fess Parker played him

Young Dillinger (1965), or How I Succeeded in Crime Without Really Trying

Young Jesse James (1960), building the infamous legend

Young Mr. Lincoln (1939), the famous full moon trial and all

Young Mr. Pitt (1942), about politics in the early nineteenth century

Young Tom Edison (1940), before he saw the light

Young Winston (1972), his rise to political note

and most astonishing of all: *Young Attila* (1971), with honorable mention to *Butch and Sundance: The Early Years* (1979)

LANDMARK ACTION

World-famous landmarks which serve as the sites for key scenes in motion pictures:

Mt. Rushmore in the climax of *North by Northwest* (1959), site of a dizzying chase

The Empire State Building in *King Kong* (1933), where the giant ape meets his doom

The Eiffel Tower in *Superman II* (1981), as the tourist attraction is taken by terrorists

The Golden Gate Bridge in *Superman* (1978), saved from collapsing during an earthquake

The Washington Monument in *The Deadly Mantis* (1957), as the prehistoric insect lights upon it

Devil's Tower in *Close Encounters of the Third Kind* (1977), the mountainous landmark designated by aliens as a landing area

Big Ben in *Konga* (1961), before whose clock face the giant ape is gunned down

The Tower Bridge in *Gorgo* (1961), smashed by the titanic beast

The Colosseum in *Twenty Million Miles to Earth* (1957), from which a giant Venusian is shot

The Capitol in *Earth vs. the Flying Saucers* (1956), its dome and one wing smashed by flying saucers

The Statue of Liberty in *Saboteur* (1942), as said malfeasant plummets to his death from Miss Liberty's torch

The Great Pyramid of Cheops in *The Spy Who Loved*

Me (1977), beside which James Bond must fend off Soviet hirelings

The Canals of Venice in *Moonraker* (1979), where Agent 007 must elude speedboat-driving assassins in his supercharged gondola

NO RELATION

Movies that have the same title, but nothing else to do with one another:

The Island

The 1961 motion picture is a Japanese work about a family living on a tiny island. The 1980 edition was Peter Benchley's tale of modern-day pirates.

Heaven Can Wait

The 1943 version was about a man's battle to enter hell; the Warren Beatty film, from 1978, was a remake of *Here Comes Mr. Jordan* (1941).

Dressed to Kill

Brian DePalma's chilling 1980 movie had no relation whatsoever to the Basil Rathbone Sherlock Holmes opus from 1946.

Carrie

Once again, Mr. DePalma's 1976 film version of Stephen King's novel was unrelated to the William Wyler film of 1952. Wyler's film was about a farm girl; De-Palma's, a girl with telekinetic powers.

Coming-Out Party

1934 and 1962: one a love story, the other about POWs.

Black Sunday

Witches in 1960, terrorists in 1977. The witches, incidentally, made for a better motion picture.

The Warriors

An Errol Flynn costume adventure in 1955; a teen-gang flick in 1979.

Taxi

Cab wars with James Cagney in 1932; comedy with Dan Dailey in 1953.

Pretty Baby
Prostitution in the hands of Louis Malle (1978); romantic fluff in 1950.

Once a Thief
In 1950, June Havoc played a kleptomaniac. Fifteen years later, an ex-con gets wrapped up in a fresh crime.

The Turning Point
A corrupt crime committee in 1952, and the ballet in 1977.

Million Dollar Legs
W. C. Fields comedy set in the nation of Klopstokia and surrounding the Olympics in 1932; horse racing and Betty Grable were the substance of the 1939 edition.

The Wild Party
Anthony Quinn as an ex-football player in 1956, giving way to James Coco as a flamboyant, slightly sleazy actor in 1975.

Shock Treatment
A mental institution in 1964 and a *different* kind of mental institution eighteen years later: the sequel to *Rocky Horror Picture Show*.

Monkey Business
The Marx Brothers go for a cruise in 1931; Cary Grant invents a "fountain of youth" serum twenty-one years later.

Love Story
Though the dying Ali MacGraw of 1970 is better known, an unaffiliated film in 1944 featured a dying pianist and a blind pilot.

A Night to Remember
The sinking of the Titanic in the 1958 film, a murder mystery fifteen years before.

Let's Do It Again

About as striking a difference as one will find: a "screwball" musical in 1953, starring Ray Milland—and an all-black sequel to *Uptown Saturday Night* (1974) in 1975

Golden Girl

A Civil War musical in 1951, and the story of a bionic Olympic athlete in 1979.

TYPECASTING

Nonactors who were hired to play, in films, what they are in real life:

Neil Diamond as a singer in *The Jazz Singer* (1980)

Pelé as a soccer player in *Victory* (1981)

Evel Knievel as a daredevil in *Viva Knievel* (1977)

Roger Marris and Mickey Mantle as baseball players in *Safe at Home!* (1962)

Liberace as a pianist in *Sincerely Yours* (1955)

Muhammad Ali as a boxer (himself) in *The Greatest* (1977)

Jackie Robinson as Jackie Robinson in *The Jackie Robinson Story* (1950)

CATASTROPHE!

Real-life disasters dramatized by motion pictures:

The Hindenburg (1975): Robert Wise's underrated speculation as to why the German zeppelin exploded in 1937 as it attempted a landing in Lakehurst, New Jersey. The film concluded with actual footage of the crash, intercut with spectacular new scenes.

Krakatoa, East of Java (1969): Cinerama put audiences right smack in the center of the 1883 eruption, one of the most devastating volcanic upheavals in history. The film's special effects won an Oscar nomination.

A Night to Remember (1958) and *Titanic* (1953): Two superb pictures about the sinking of the unsinkable luxury liner in 1912.

The Johnstown Flood (1926): A silent film epic about the 1889 deluge, which killed more than two thousand people.

San Francisco (1936): The classic film about the quake and fire that did $524 million worth of damage in 1906.

In Old Chicago (1938): Tyrone Power vehicle about the awesome 1871 fire, from the antsy cow of Mrs. O'Leary to the heroic aftermath.

The Last Days of Pompeii (1935 and 1960): The earlier movie the better by far in the recreation of events which destroyed the city at the foot of Mt. Vesuvius in A.D. 79.

THE DEVIL, YOU SAY!

Actors who have played Lucifer or his devils in motion pictures:

Bill Cosby replete with horns, goat shanks, and red flesh in *The Devil and Max Devlin* (1981)

Peter Cook (Dudley Moore's partner) in *Bedazzled* (1967) as Mephisto

Walter Huston as a cigar-chomping devil in *All That Money Can Buy* (1940), here called Mr. Scratch

Laird Cregar as Satan in *Heaven Can Wait* (1943)

Claude Rains as Satan in *Angel on My Shoulder* (1946)—this, not long after he had played an angel in *Here Comes Mr. Jordan* (1941)

Ray Milland as Satan in *Alias Nick Beal* (1949)

Stanley Holloway in *Meet Mr. Lucifer* (1953)

Ray Walston as Beelzebub in *Damn Yankees* (1958)

Andre Teuber as Mephistopheles in *Dr. Faustus* (1967)

Vincent Price in *The Story of Mankind* (1957)

Donald Pleasance in *The Greatest Story Ever Told* (1965)

Stig Jarrel in *The Devil's Eye* (1960)

Rex Ingram in *Cabin in the Sky* (1943)

Vittorio Gassman in *The Devil in Love* (1966)

Ralph Richardson in *Tales from the Crypt* (1972)

SUPERMEN

Actors with an inordinate amount of courage: they stepped into parts hard upon the heels of actors who were synonymous with the roles:

Roger Moore: Sean Connery had played James Bond in six films, which ranked among the most popular ever made. So closely identified with the part was Connery, in fact, that no other film he made came close to matching the box office of the 007 adventures. Though many people still prefer Connery in the part, the five Moore Bonds have taken in more money by far than those of Connery. It is reported, however, that before beginning each Bond film, even today, the producers approach Connery to play the part.

Lex Barker: There have been few motion-picture series as popular as the Tarzan saga, a part which Johnny Weissmuller made his own in twelve films. Curiously, he was nothing like the Tarzan whose adventures were chronicled by Edgar Rice Burroughs in two dozen books—a barely articulate savage as opposed to a cultured English lord. Nonetheless, the public loved Weissmuller, and when he left the part after seventeen years in a salary dispute, Barker moved in. Five films later, he moved out when the producers demanded a multipicture contract, while he would settle for nothing more than per-picture deals.

Glenn Strange: Oddly enough, though Strange played the part of the Frankenstein Monster immediately after Boris Karloff had given three classic performances as the creature, it is Strange's face which is most *familiar* as the artificial man. Toys, ads, T-shirts, and the like which license the likeness from Universal Pictures almost invariably take the harsher, more angular Strange face. There is nothing to compare in the matter of the performances, though this is not the fault of Strange. The scripts for the three Karloff vehicles were infinitely meatier than for Strange's trilogy, the last of which was *Abbott and Costello Meet Frankenstein* (1948).

John Wayne: It doesn't exactly take courage for a superstar to step into a part identified with a lesser name. However, that doesn't guarantee absolute acceptance. After playing Davy Crockett in three films, Fess Parker *became* the American hero in the mind of the public (aided by constant exposure on the Disney TV series). Thus, when John Wayne was the next to play the legendary patriot in *The Alamo* (1960), what he was playing was John Wayne and not Crockett. Still, Wayne had the charisma to overcome these roadblocks and give one of his better performances.

Roland Winters: It was gutsy enough for Sidney Toler to take over the role of Charlie Chan from Warner Oland upon the actor's death. Oland had left behind sixteen films about the Oriental sleuth. But Toler moved in and actually exceeded the output of his predecessor, making twenty-two Chan flicks. Unfortunately, Toler clearly lost interest toward the end, and his latter features were not very good. Thus, when Winters came on with Toler's death, he inherited not only a closely identified part but a failing series. Nonetheless, he carried on nobly in six features which, alas, in the script and production department gave him virtually no support.

Alan Arkin: To step into the shoes of Peter Sellers is no easy task. But Arkin did so, playing Inspector Clouseau in a 1968 film of the same name. Sellers had defined the part brilliantly in *The Pink Panther* (1964) and *A Shot in the Dark* (1964), and indeed returned to it in three subsequent films. Arkin was not helped by a script which was markedly inferior to those of the earlier films; Sellers overcame inadequate writing in the last three films with his unparalleled comic genius. Sellers was planning to play Clouseau yet again at the time of his death. Dudley Moore has been tentatively named to take the part.

STACKING UP

It's a familiar axiom in Hollywood that sequels are rarely if ever as good as the originals. To determine whether or not that is a fair generalization, we've gone to original reviews of the following films. Per film, up to 35 journals, magazines, and newspapers were consulted, sources which had reviewed *all* versions. With 100% being the consensus that the movie was excellent, 0% that it was an out-and-out bomb, here are the results:

Mutiny on the Bounty: 97% for 1935, 45% for 1962

Tarzan, the Ape Man: 87% for 1932, 12% for 1959, 2% for 1981

The Hound of the Baskervilles: 78% for 1939, 55% for 1959

King Kong: 93% for 1933, 31% for 1976

Stagecoach: 90% for 1939, 25% for 1966

The Lost World: 95% for 1925, 17% for 1960

Dracula: 95% for 1931, 40% for 1979

The Charge of the Light Brigade: 75% for 1936, 65% for 1968

Ben-Hur: 85% for 1926, 100% for 1959

The Jazz Singer: 80% for 1953, 10% for 1980 (Note: the 1927 original cannot be considered by virtue of the novelty of being the first sound film, which drew most of the press; surprisingly, not all of that press was favorable, the film rating only 62%)

The Thief of Bagdad: 78% for 1924, 90% for 1940, 20% for 1961

The 39 Steps: 90% in 1935, 29% in 1960, 8% in 1979

Julius Caesar: 88% in 1953, 24% in 1971

Cleopatra: 70% in 1934, 30% in 1963

A Star Is Born: 85% in 1937, 90% in 1954, 32% in 1976

Treasure Island: 91% in 1934, 89% in 1950 (Disney)

Characters who are pitifully and hopelessly drunk on screen:

Arthur (1981): Dudley Moore as a young man who stands to inherit $750 million if he'll marry. The girl in question wants him to control his drinking, which is out of the question for the youthful millionaire.

The Lost Weekend (1945): Ray Milland won an Oscar as an alcoholic.

Too Much, Too Soon (1958): Errol Flynn as John Barrymore, portrayed as a drunk.

The Bad and the Beautiful (1952): Lana Turner as Georgia Lorrison, an actress and a lush.

Magnificent Obsession (1935): Robert Taylor as Bobby Merrick, a playboy whose drunk attack on a woman causes her to be run over by a car.

Nightmare Alley (1947): Tyrone Power as Stan Carlisle, an opportunist who becomes a mentalist and tries to blackmail the patients of an equally fraudulent psychologist. In the end, Carlisle is reduced to a drunk who appears as a geek in a circus, performing for booze.

Who's Afraid of Virginia Woolf? (1966): Liz Taylor as Martha, Richard Burton as George, George Segal as Nick, and Sandy Dennis as Honey—*all* drinking it up in this film version of Edward Albee's play.

Wuthering Heights (1939): Young, wealthy Hindley (Hugh Williams) abuses poor young Heathcliff (Laurence Olivier); when in later years the roles are reversed, Hindley dependent upon Heathcliff for the roof over his head, the destroyed soul turns to the bottle.

BIG BOOZERS (continued)

The Pilot (1979): Cliff Robertson as a sodden airline pilot.

Madame X (1966): Lana Turner again, this time as Holly Parker, a woman who degenerates from wealth to drink and prostitution.

The Sun Also Rises (1957): Errol Flynn as Mike Campbell, Hemingway's drunken member of the "lost generation." One of the actor's finest performances, and one of his last.

The Most Dangerous Game (1932): In a fine supporting role, Robert Armstrong plays a soused young man who dies on the island of the mad Count Zaroff, who hunts humans as game.

Moulin Rouge (1952): José Ferrer as Toulouse-Lautrec, the nineteenth-century painter who imbibed the deadly absinthe.

Two Weeks in Another Town (1962): Kirk Douglas as Jack Andrus, an actor who has been ruined by alcohol.

Days of Wine and Roses (1962): Lee Remick was Oscar-nominated for her part as a woman driven to drink.

EMCEES

Celebrities who have hosted the Oscar ceremonies:

Lionel Barrymore (1932)
Will Rogers (1933)
George Jessel (1936)
Bob Hope (1939, 1944, 1945 [co-host], 1952 [co-host], 1954 [co-host], 1957 [co-host], 1958 [co-host], 1959, 1960, 1961, 1964, 1965, 1966, 1967, 1974 [co-host], 1977)
Johnny Carson (1978, 1979, 1980)
Jack Benny (1943, 1946)
Jimmy Stewart (1945 [co-host], 1957 [co-host])
Robert Montgomery (1948)
Fred Astaire (1950)
Danny Kaye (1951)
Conrad Nagel (1952 [co-host])
Donald O'Connor (1953 [co-host])
Fredric March (1953 [co-host])
Thelma Ritter (1954 [co-host])
Jerry Lewis (1955 [co-host], 1956 [co-host], 1958)
Claudette Colbert (1955 [co-host])
Celeste Holm (1956 [co-host])
David Niven (1957 [co-host], 1958 [co-host], 1973 [co-host])
Rosalind Russell (1957 [co-host])
Tony Randall (1958 [co-host])
Laurence Olivier (1958 [co-host])
Frank Sinatra (1962, 1974 [co-host])
Jack Lemmon (1963, 1971 [co-host])
Helen Hayes (1971 [co-host])
Alan King (1971 [co-host])

EMCEES (continued)

Sammy Davis, Jr. (1971 [co-host], 1974 [co-host])
Carol Burnett (1972 [co-host])
Charlton Heston (1972 [co-host])
Rock Hudson (1972 [co-host])
Michael Caine (1972 [co-host])
Diana Ross (1973 [co-host])
Burt Reynolds (1973 [co-host])
Shirley MacLaine (1974 [co-host])]
Goldie Hawn (1975 [co-host])
Gene Kelly (1975 [co-host])
Walter Matthau (1975 [co-host])
George Segal (1975 [co-host])
Robert Shaw (1975 [co-host])
Warren Beatty (1976 [co-host])
Ellen Burstyn (1976 [co-host])
Jane Fonda (1976 [co-host])
Richard Pryor (1976 [co-host])

ENCORE!

Music that was so good, it appeared in more than one picture:

Alexander Nevsky (1938): The original score for this Russian masterpiece was composed by Sergei Prokofiev. Woody Allen used portions of the music for his own Russian saga, *Love and Death* (1975).

Son of Frankenstein (1939): Frank Skinner's music was so evocative in this Boris Karloff-Basil Rathbone horror film that it was reused in their next, unrelated teaming, *The Tower of London*, later that year.

Quo Vadis (1951): Miklos Rozsa was so enamored of a march he composed for this MGM Roman spectacle that, eight years later, he reused it in that studio's *Ben-Hur*.

Superman (1978): John Williams' score for this monumental comic book was reorchestrated by Ken Thorne and mingled with new material for *Superman II* (1981).

Star Wars (1977): The popular main theme returned in *The Empire Strikes Back* (1980) and will be heard yet again in *Revenge of the Jedi* (1983).

Bride of Frankenstein (1935): Franz Waxman's brilliant score was used in a parade of motion-picture serials and low-budget action pictures throughout the 1940s, most notably in *Flash Gordon* (1936) and *Buck Rogers* (1939).

The Adventures of Don Juan (1948): Max Steiner's stirring music stirred the makers of *Zorro, the Gay Blade* (1981) to rerecord the score for their film.

Lawrence of Arabia (1962): This one is pure homage, as Marvin Hamlisch used the famous "Desert Theme" in *The Spy Who Loved Me* (1977) when James Bond crosses a desert.

SEX CHANGE

Movies wherein a woman plays what is traditionally a man's role:

Miss Robin Crusoe (1954): Amanda Blake alone on an uncharted island

Dr. Jekyll and Sister Hyde (1971): Ralph Bates turns into Martine Beswick

The Incredible Shrinking Woman (1980): Lily Tomlin as the character who was a male in the Richard Matheson novel *The Shrinking Man* and in the 1957 movie *The Incredible Shrinking Man*

Woman They Almost Lynched (1953): a lady gunslinger

She-Wolf of London (1946): move over Lon Chaney, Jr.

Sheba Baby (1975): black woman as a detective

Frankenstein's Daughter (1959); a female heir of the ambitious doctor

The Wild World of Batwoman (1966): unauthorized spinoff of Batman character

Lady in the Iron Mask (1952): Dumas rewritten

Lady Scarface (1941): Capone's got nothing on her

The Wife of Monte Cristo (1946) and *The Countess of Monte Cristo* (1948): Dumas undone once more

Unusual ways which people have flown in motion pictures:

Mary Poppins (1964): holding an open umbrella

Chitty Chitty Bang Bang (1968): a flying car

First Men in the Moon (1965): "Cavorite," a paint which cuts off the pull of gravity

Clash of the Titans (1981): Perseus gets around on the back of Pegasus, the winged horse

Peter Pan (1954): a pinch of magic dust gets Wendy and the kids off the ground

The Wizard of Oz (1939): Dorothy is swept up inside a tornado

Abbott and Costello Meet Frankenstein (1948): Dracula, one of the film's many monsters, turns into a bat

Dr. Strangelove (1964): Slim Pickens, as a bomber pilot, rides an atom bomb

Willy Wonka and the Chocolate Factory (1971): visitors to same gurgle down a special soda pop whose gaseous content causes them to rise

Superman (1978): under his own steam, due to the less inhibiting nature of our world's yellow sun as opposed to the red one of his native planet

The Thief of Bagdad (1940): Sabu rides around on a flying carpet

The Seventh Voyage of Sinbad (1958): the Arabian Knight is hauled to a mountaintop in the talons of an enormous, two-headed roc

Modern Problems (1981): Chevy Chase levitates himself through telekinesis

The Absent Minded Professor (1961): many characters

bounced through the air by "flubber," which is flying rubber

Dreams of the Rarebit Fiend (1906): John Brawn zips through the skies over Brooklyn holding onto the footboard of his airborne bed

The Little Prince (1974): the Prince soars through the air wrapped in ribbons borne aloft by birds

Scrooge (1971): a stingy Ebenezer is dragged through the air by the ghost of Jacob Marley, and subsequently by other specters

DIDJA KNOW . . .

*Harrison Ford was not the first choice to play Indiana Jones in *Raiders of the Lost Ark* (1981). The producers wanted actor Tom Selleck, but he was tied up with his new TV series *Magnum P.I.*

*The most expensive film Errol Flynn ever appeared in was not one of his spectacular swashbucklers . . . but *The Sun Also Rises* (1957), which cost $5,000,000 due to location filming all over Mexico.

*Kirk Douglas, Richard Burton, Peter O'Toole, and Al Pacino have been nominated for close to twenty Oscars between them, but have won none.

*There have been three movies based on magazines: *Animal House* (1979), *Heavy Metal* (1981), and *Up the Academy* (1980), from *National Lampoon*, *Heavy Metal*, and *Mad* respectively. *Mad*'s film was so awful that star Ron Liebman ordered his name removed from the credits; further, after the film's initial release, *Mad* had all references to the magazine deleted in ads, in the title, in the closing credits, and most telling of all, the removal of all footage showing the *Mad* mascot Alfred E. Newman in the flesh.

*Noel Neill, who played Lois Lane on the Superman TV series, is seen briefly as Lois Lane's mother in *Superman* (1978). Lois' father is played momentarily by Kirk Alyn, who limned the role of Superman in two movie serials.

*Sophia Loren refused to wear "aging" makeup in *El Cid* (1962), looking eternally youthful while film hubby Charlton Heston adds decades.

*Legendary science-fiction author H. G. Wells actually wrote a screenplay solely for motion pictures, not based on any of his novels: it was *The Man Who Could Work Miracles* (1937), about a store clerk who is given supreme power by the gods.

*Boris Karloff was already forty-four years of age when he took the part of the Frankenstein monster in the 1931 film—a role Bela Lugosi had turned down because he would be seen but not heard. Karloff had already been an actor in films for twelve years.

*As a footnote to Mr. Karloff, he played the role of the monster for the third and last time in *Son of Frankenstein* (1939). He did the job with a broken hip, having smashed it at the commencement of shooting.

AN EXAMPLE TO US ALL

Motion pictures about people who have had to confront severe handicaps:

The Miracle Worker (1962): Patty Duke as the blind and deaf Helen Keller, with Anne Bancroft as her teacher. Both won Oscars for their performances.

The Best Years of Our Lives (1946): Harold Russell won an Oscar for his portrayal of a handless WWII veteran. Russell, not a professional actor, is himself handless. The picture was named Best of the Year by the Academy of Motion Picture Arts and Sciences.

Coming Home (1978): Jon Voight as a paraplegic survivor of Vietnam, at first cared for and then loved by Jane Fonda. A multiple Oscar winner, including Voight.

The Other Side of the Mountain (1975): Olympic-bound skier Jill Kinmont (Marilyn Hassett) is paralyzed in an accident and must learn to cope with her handicap. A sequel was released three years later.

A Patch of Blue (1965): Elizabeth Hartman as a blind white girl who falls in love with a black man (Sidney Poitier).

Charly (1968): Charly Gordon (Cliff Robertson) is a retardate who is turned into a genius by an experimental operation—then reverts. Charly's methods of dealing with life before his operation are touching, and his reversion is heart-shattering. Robertson won Best Actor of the Year. A sequel, *Charly II,* began filming in 1980 but folded when funds ran out. Robertson hopes to continue at a later date.

Magnificent Obsession (1935): Though it is Irene Dunne who is blinded when run over by a car—it is Robert

Taylor who has the greater albatross. His irresponsibility caused the accident, and he spends his time transforming himself from playboy to surgeon to help her.

Follow the Sun (1951): The true story of golfer Ben Hogan (Glenn Ford), who returned to the green as a champion after being crippled in a car accident.

BEHIND THE SCREEN

Books about the making of motion pictures (*not* simply the script in book form):

The Making of Kubrick's 2001 by Jerome Agel, New American Library

The Making of Superman by David Petrou, Warner Books

The Making of Star Trek the Motion Picture by Susan Sackett, Wallaby

Chekov's Enterprise: A Journal of the Making of Star Trek by Walter Koenig, Pocket Books

Once Upon a Galaxy: A Journal of the Making of The Empire Strikes Back by Alan Arnold, Del Rey/Ballantine

Down the Yellow Brick Road: The Making of The Wizard of Oz by Doug McClelland, Pyramid

The Animated Raggedy Ann and Andy: The Story Behind the Movie by John Canemaker, Bobbs-Merrill

The Creation of Dino de Laurentiis' King Kong by Bruce Bahrenburg, Pocket Books

The Making of King Kong (the 1933 original) by Goldner and Turner, A. S. Barnes

The Jaws Log by Carl Gottlieb, Dell

The Jaws 2 Log by Ray Loynd, Dell

The Making of the Exorcist II: The Heretic by Barbara Pallenberg, Warner Books

Scarlett, Rhett, and a Cast of Thousands by Roland Flamini, Macmillan

Beauty and the Beast: Diary of a Film by Jean Cocteau

Close Encounters of the Third Kind Diary by Bob Balaban, Paradise

BEHIND THE SCREEN (continued)

The Citizen Kane Book by Pauline Kael, Little, Brown

On the Set of Fellini's Satyricon: A Behind-the-Scenes Diary by Eileen Lanouette Hughes, Morrow

On Making a Movie: Brewster McCloud by C. K. McClelland, New American Library

The Meteor Scrapbook by Bernhardt J. Hurwood, Grosset and Dunlap

The Wiz Scrapbook by Richard Anobile, Berkley/Windhover

Roger Moore's James Bond Diary (Live and Let Die) by Roger Moore, Fawcett

The *Focus On . . .* series: *Bonnie and Clyde, Shoot the Piano Player, Rashomon, Citizen Kane, Blow-Up, The Seventh Seal,* and *The Birth of a Nation,* Prentice-Hall

Filmguide to Psycho by James Naremore, Indiana University

The Story Behind the Exorcist by Travers and Reiff, Crown

The Two Hundred Days of 8½ by Deena Boyer, Macmillan

The Book of Alien by Scanlon and Gross, Simon & Schuster

Notes (Apocalypse Now) by Eleanor Coppola, Simon and Schuster

The Making of Raiders of the Lost Ark by Derek Taylor, Ballantine

BEST PICTURE . . . AND
BETTER PICTURE

Here's a list of the pictures that have been awarded the Oscar as best . . . and, where appropriate, the films that lost yet whose luster equals or surpasses that of the winner:

1928: *Wings*

1929: *Broadway Melody*

1930: *All Quiet on the Western Front*

1931: *Cimarron* (loser: *The Front Page*)

1932: *Grand Hotel* (loser: *The Champ*)

1933: *Cavalcade* (loser: *The Private Life of Henry VIII*)

1934: *It Happened One Night* (loser: *The Thin Man*)

1935: *Mutiny on the Bounty* (loser: *The Informer*)

1936: *The Great Ziegfeld*

1937: *The Life of Emile Zola*

1938: *You Can't Take it With You* (loser: *The Adventures of Robin Hood*)

1939: *Gone With the Wind* (losers: *The Wizard of Oz, Of Mice and Men, Wuthering Heights, Mr. Smith Goes to Washington*)

1940: *Rebecca* (losers: *The Grapes of Wrath, The Great Dictator*)

1941: *How Green Was My Valley* (losers: *Citizen Kane, The Maltese Falcon*)

1942: *Mrs. Miniver* (loser: *The Magnificent Ambersons*)

1943: *Casablanca*

1944: *Going My Way*

1945: *The Lost Weekend* (loser: *Spellbound*)

1946: *The Best Years of Our Lives*

1947: *Gentleman's Agreement* (loser: *Great Expectations*)

1948: *Hamlet* (loser: *The Treasure of the Sierra Madre*)

1949: *All the King's Men*

1950: *All About Eve* (losers: *Father of the Bride, Sunset Boulevard*)

1951: *An American in Paris* (loser: *A Streetcar Named Desire*)

1952: *The Greatest Show on Earth* (loser: *High Noon*)

1953: *From Here to Eternity* (loser: *Shane*)

1954: *On the Waterfront*

1955: *Marty* (loser: *Mister Roberts*)

1956: *Around the World in 80 Days* (losers: *The Ten Commandments, Giant, The King and I, Friendly Persuasion*)

1957: *The Bridge on the River Kwai*

1958: *Gigi*

1959: *Ben-Hur*

1960: *The Apartment* (loser: *Elmer Gantry*)

1961: *West Side Story*

1962: *Lawrence of Arabia* (losers: *The Longest Day, To Kill a Mockingbird*)

1963: *Tom Jones* (losers: *How the West Was Won, America, America*)

1964: *My Fair Lady* (losers: *Dr. Strangelove, Becket, Mary Poppins*)

1965: *The Sound of Music* (losers: *Dr. Zhivago, Ship of Fools*)

1966: *A Man for All Seasons* (loser: *Who's Afraid of Virginia Woolf?*)

1967: *In the Heat of the Night* (losers: *Guess Who's Coming to Dinner, The Graduate*)

1968: *Oliver* (losers: *The Lion in Winter, Romeo and Juliet*)

1969: *Midnight Cowboy* (losers: *Butch Cassidy and the Sundance Kid, Z, Anne of the Thousand Days*)

1970: *Patton* (losers: *M*A*S*H, Five Easy Pieces*)

1971: *The French Connection* (losers: *A Clockwork Orange, The Last Picture Show, Fiddler on the Roof*)

1972: *The Godfather* (losers: *Cabaret, Sounder, Deliverance*)

1973: *The Sting* (losers: *The Exorcist, Cries and Whispers*)

1974: *The Godfather Part II* (losers: *Lenny, The Conversation*)

1975: *One Flew Over the Cuckoo's Nest* (losers: *Jaws, Nashville*)

1976: *Rocky* (losers: *Network, Taxi Driver*)

1977: *Annie Hall*

1978: *The Deer Hunter* (losers: *Coming Home, An Unmarried Woman*)

1979: *Kramer vs. Kramer* (losers: *All That Jazz, Apocalypse Now*)

1980: *Ordinary People* (loser: *Raging Bull*)

COME BACK, SHANE

Alan Ladd, alas, is gone—but there are many actors who have by and large retired from films with a good many roles yet to play. For their fans, and for the industry, the following should be arm-twisted by some ambitious producer:

Cary Grant
Victor Mature
Richard Widmark
Terry-Thomas
Paul Scofield
Sidney Poitier
Deborah Kerr
Danny Kaye
Julie Harris
Yul Brynner
Brigitte Bardot
Gina Lollobrigida
Steve Reeves
Cornel Wilde
Jane Wyman
Gordon MacRae

CAN'T STOP AT ONE

Films in which the star played two or more diverse roles:

Mary Poppins (1964): Dick Van Dyke as Burt the Chimney Sweep and an aged bank president

The Ten Commandments (1956): Charlton Heston as Moses and as the voice of God

Which Way Is Up? (1978): Richard Pryor as a farm worker, his father, and a preacher

The Seven Faces of Dr. Lao (1964): Tony Randall as a blind seer, an ancient Chinese, Medusa, Pan, the Abominable Snowman, and Merlin (the seventh face wasn't his)

Dr. Strangelove (1964): Peter Sellers, as he did in a number of films, played several parts, that of the President of the United States, a British officer, and the mad Dr. Strangelove

Man of La Mancha (1972): Peter O'Toole as Cervantes, Alonso Quijana, and Don Quixote

Oh Heavenly Dog (1980): Chevy Chase as a detective and as the voice of Benji

Bride of Frankenstein (1935): Elsa Lanchester as the monster's wife and as Mary Shelley, author of *Frankenstein*, in a clever prologue

The Wizard of Oz (1939): Margaret Hamilton, Frank Morgan, Ray Bolger, Bert Lahr, and Jack Haley all played dual roles as Kansas folk and denizens of Oz

Dr. Jekyll and Mr. Hyde (1932): Fredric March as the titular persons, a dual role essayed by others, including Spencer Tracy in 1941

The Secret Life of Walter Mitty (1947): Danny Kaye daydreams about being other people, with lives more exciting than his own as a proofreader at a magazine firm

Plaza Suite (1971): Three different stories, with Walter Matthau donning a different mantle in each

The Wonderful World of the Brothers Grimm (1962): Laurence Harvey played both fairy-tale anthologist Wilhelm Grimm and the featured figure in one of his fairy tales, "The Cobbler and the Elves"

NO, THANKS . . . AGAIN

In our previous volume, we listed actors who have turned down roles for sundry reasons. Here are more:

Christopher Reeve refused a fee of $1,000,000 to star in *American Gigolo* (1980), a part which went to Richard Gere.

Albert Finney turned down the role of *Lawrence of Arabia* (1962), the film which made an international star of Peter O'Toole.

Shirley MacLaine decided she didn't really need $1,000,000 and said no to *Casino Royale* (1967)

Charlton Heston nixed *The Omen* (1976), and Gregory Peck made a comeback with the film.

Frank Sinatra wasn't satisfied with the fee he was offered to do *The Little Prince* (1974), so Broadway's "Don Quixote," Richard Kiley, played the Pilot in the picture.

George Segal didn't like the way Blake Edwards was handling *10*, so he took a hike—launching Dudley Moore into stardom.

Laurence Olivier decided, for creative reasons, to bow out of *Judgment at Nuremburg* (1961), giving Burt Lancaster a plum supporting role.

Warren Beatty can be thanked for Robert Redford's popularity: Beatty turned down *Butch Cassidy and the Sundance Kid* (1969). The producers had been ready to offer him either role.

Frank Sinatra quit *The Only Game in Town* (1969), which was being directed by the legendary George Stevens. This is the film Beatty did in lieu of *Butch Cas-*

sidy and the Sundance Kid. One was a smash hit, while the other sank. That's show biz, as they say. . . .

Rex Harrison did not want to play Ebenezer Scrooge . . . nor did Richard Harris. So Albert Finney took the part in the 1971 musical *Scrooge*, adding to his too-meager list of performances on film.

Richard Dreyfuss couldn't get along with director Bob Fosse, so Roy Scheider slipped into *All That Jazz* (1980), a box-office giant, and earned himself a well-deserved Oscar nomination.

PEOPLE TO KNOW

You won't find these names in *People* Magazine—but they have done more to shape the film industry than any half-dozen top stars. This is not a history lesson; simply an appreciation of genius known primarily to people in the film industry:

Pare Lorentz: An early movie critic, in the era of the silents, and a fighter against censorship. Career enough for anyone, but Lorentz went on to become one of film history's greatest documentary moviemakers. Among his greatest works are *The Plow That Broke the Plains* (1936) and *The River* (1937).

F. W. Murnau: A German actor-turned-director who, in the 1920s and 30s, made a number of ground-breaking motion pictures. His expressionistic horror film *Janus-Faced* (1920) is one, but *The Last Laugh* (1924), one of the most moving films ever made, and *Sunrise* (1927), one of the most surreal and beautiful, are his masterworks.

Sergei Eisenstein: Although D. W. Griffith and, of late, Abel Gance *(Napoleon)* have been getting all the credit for inventing most of the techniques used in modern filmmaking, this Russian director achieved passion and scope in epic films unmatched by *any* director. His most famous works, brilliant even by today's standards, are *Potemkin* (1925) and *Alexander Nevsky* (1938), the latter quite possibly the most stirring film of all time.

Joseph Ruttenberg: Shifting from the cinema gods to a mere genius, Ruttenberg is one of the most famous cinematographers for women in Hollywood history.

From Lana Turner on down, he knows how to make a lady look her best.

David Lean: Everyone praises the young directors, the George Lucas and Steven Spielbergs, and if performance is any measure, they *deserve* the tens of millions of dollars they get to make their diverting little epics. But Lean, who has made classic after classic, has been unemployed for over a decade. After such masterpieces as *The Bridge on the River Kwai* (1957), *Lawrence of Arabia* (1962), *Breaking the Sound Barrier* (1952), *Great Expectations* (1947), and many more, the kid deserves another chance. His last project, an aborted *Mutiny on the Bounty* starring Christopher Reeve, was canceled in 1979 after the *Bounty* had been built but nothing photographed.

ONCE IS USUALLY ENOUGH

Actors who have gone behind the camera to direct a motion picture, while at the same time *starring* in it . . . with less-than-satisfactory results:

Antony and Cleopatra (1972): Charlton Heston's first directorial effort, a project he undertook when Laurence Olivier and Orson Welles weren't able to do it. Heston also starred. The film was never released in the United States. His most recent film, *Mother Lode*, was also directed by its star.

Panic in the Year Zero (1962): This interesting if low, low budget film was directed by Ray Milland, who also toplined. It portrayed the aftermath of a nuclear war, and its impact on one family which headed for the hills.

J. W. Coop (1972): An exception to the rule as Cliff Robertson wrote, directed, and starred in a brilliant film about a rodeo rider. It was, alas, a commercial flop. Robertson also directed *The Pilot* in 1979, though the film has yet to be released. His production of *Charly II*, on which he was writer-director-star, collapsed a few days into filming when financing failed to come through.

The Alamo (1960): It's impossible not to like this top-heavy but spirited film, directed by and starring John Wayne. However, *The Green Berets*, made eight years later, with Wayne again serving as director and star, is painfully bad.

The Kentuckian (1955): Burt Lancaster's enormously underrated western film, with Lancaster as helmer and star.

ONCE IS USUALLY ENOUGH (continued)

Scalawag (1973) and *Posse* (1975): Kirk Douglas behind and before the camera. The first is tolerable, the second better. Both flopped.

Play Misty For Me (1971): Clint Eastwood has gone behind the camera with creatively more satisfying results than most. However, neither this film nor *Bronco Billy* (1980) was a hit, despite his presence as star.

It's Always Fair Weather (1955): Directed by and co-starring Gene Kelly, one of the star's lesser vehicles as an actor. His direction, however, is fine.

The Savage Is Loose (1974): George C. Scott not only starred in and directed this disaster, he produced and *distributed* it as well, theater to theater.

One-Eyed Jacks (1961): Marlon Brando surprised a great many doubters by directing an engrossing, if slightly pretentious western. He proved that he is one director who can get Marlon Brando's cooperation as an actor.

The Naked Prey (1966) and *Beach Red* (1967): Two superb movies that make one wish Cornel Wilde had directed more of his own starring vehicles.

None but the Brave (1965): Frank Sinatra produced, directed, and starred in this Pacific war film. The talented Mr. Sinatra spread himself just a bit thin here.

Billy Budd (1962): Peter Ustinov's superb version of the classic Herman Melville novel. He was both director and co-star, as well, of *Hammersmith Is Out* (1972).

Hamlet (1948): There's nothing Lord Laurence Olivier doesn't do brilliantly. He happened to star in and direct this classic.

Dr. Faustus (1968): Richard Burton's unjustly condemned fantasy. He'd have done better, though, with another director directing him.

Charlie Bubbles (1968): Albert Finney helming Albert

Finney as a philandering writer in an unjustly overlooked movie.

The Ceremony (1962): Laurence Harvey, an unjustly maligned actor, unfortunately deserved the pie-in-the-face he got for directing and acting in this tale of a man indebted to his brother for saving his life.

The World's Greatest Lover (1977): The pundits say that Gene Wilder is nothing without Mel Brooks, and vice versa; Wilder's talent, as evidenced by this and other films, is clearly the more even and inventive. An overlooked film about the search for the new Valentino, with Wilder applying for the job.

A Warm December (1973): In subsequent films, such as *Uptown Saturday Night* (1974), Sidney Poitier proved that he can both direct and act in one film. This rehash of *Love Story* is not such an example.

Citizen Kane (1940): Like Laurence Olivier, Orson Welles is an exception; virtually no one but Welles can get as brilliant a performance from the actor as Welles. This one, of course, and also *Lady from Shanghai* (1948) and *Touch of Evil* (1958).

Three on a Couch (1966): It's fashionable to slam Jerry Lewis, but he's a better actor/director than most. Better yet, his pictures are entertaining.

The Seduction of Joe Tynan (1978): Alan Alda stretching his much-lauded creative muscles and proving that what plays well on TV is hammy on the big screen. He needs a director other than himself.

30 (1959): Jack Webb directing Jack Webb directing a great metropolitan newspaper. Routine but Webbishly gritty.

Husbands (1970): The always-interesting John Cassavetes directed himself, along with Peter Falk and Ben Gazzara, in this tale of a "midlife crisis" for a trio of friends.

ONCE IS USUALLY ENOUGH (continued)

The Last Movie (1971): Shooting star Dennis Hopper did himself in by jack-of-all-trading this failure on the heels of his successful *Easy Rider* (1969), which he starred in and directed.

TURNABOUT

Actors who have decided to try their hand at directing only:

The Buccaneer (1958): It must have been difficult for Cecil B. DeMille to produce a film he did not direct, but that's exactly what he did for this remake of his 1938 swashbuckling classic. This time, it was his son-in-law Anthony Quinn at the helm. Though Quinn tried hard, and did manage to bring some zest to the expository scenes, the action fell flat.

Kotch (1971): Jack Lemmon's directional debut, guiding his old partner Walter Matthau through this entertaining tale of an old gentleman's struggle for dignity.

Ordinary People (1980): Robert Redford's turn behind the cameras, an overpraised, pretentious, unbearably stagy soap opera.

Night of the Hunter (1955): Proving that he was as fine a director as he was an actor, Charles Laughton took audiences on a nightmarish roller-coaster ride through this story of lunatic Robert Mitchum menacing just about everyone in the cast as he searches for hidden loot.

Short Cut to Hell (1957): Like all of the above-mentioned actors, this was James Cagney's one stab at directing, a pedestrian gunslinger flick.

Son of Blob (1972): Believe it or not, this semisatiric sequel to *The Blob* (1958) was directed by Larry Hagman!

WHAT, ME WORRY?

One of the most successful stories in the history of magazine publishing has been the nearly three decades of the satiric *Mad*. Though its luster has been diminished somewhat in recent years by the rowdier, more scatological *National Lampoon*, its film parodies remain classics. Here are a few they've done, and done very well over the years:

Lover's Story (or, "The Old Bawl Game")

Airplot ("Mr. Bomb Carria? Oh, yes! Here we Are! Seat 17C!")

The $ound of Money ("Movie fans love all the tears that it brings/these are just some of the corniest things!")

Balmy and Clod ("We been goin' together fo' 51 bank jobs an' 112 killings! Le's make out now, Clod!")

The Poopsidedown Adventure ("My church was so cold, we didn't have Holy Water . . . we had Holy Ice!")

Put*on (or "Great Scott Department")

What's the Connection (or "Inside Dope Department")

Botch Casually and the Someduance Kid ("You look so cute with those baby blue eyes, we all thought you were Calamity Jane!")

201 Minutes of A Space Idiocy (or "Slab Schtick Comedy Department")

Superduperman ("I'm outracing a speeding locomotive!" "Big deal! This is the Long Island Railroad!")

. . . not to mention:

A Crockwork Lemon

ack, Hack Sweet Has-Been

he Sinpiper

ad *East Side Story*, the best of them all, a musical set at
  the United Nations

THE UPPER CLASSES

Europe isn't the only place with royalty; just take a look at Hollywood:

King Kong (1933)
Queen of Outer Space (1958)
Dracula, Prince of Darkness (1966)
Princess of the Nile (1954)
Countess from Hong Kong (1967)
Count of Monte Cristo (1934)
Lord Jim (1965)
Land of the Pharaohs (1955)
Emperor of the North Pole (1973)
Duke of West Point (1938)
Earl of Chicago (1940)
The Duchess and the Dirtwater Fox (1976)
Lady Caroline Lamb (1972)

ALL ASHORE

Being the many captains who, oddly named though they may often be, sailed the high seas and toplined motion pictures:

The Adventures of Captain Fabian (1951) with Errol Flynn

Captain Blood (1935), again Mr. Flynn

Captain Apache (1971) with Lee Van Cleef

Captain Carey, U.S.A. (1950) with Alan Ladd

Captain China (1949) with John Payne

Captain Eddie (1945) with Fred MacMurray

Captain Falcon (1958) with Lex Barker

Captain Fury (1939) with Brian Aherne

Captain Horatio Hornblower (1951) with Gregory Peck

Captain January (1936), starring Shirley Temple

Captain John Smith and Pocahontas (1953) with Anthony Dexter

Captain Kidd (1945) with Charles Laughton

Abbott and Costello Meet Captain Kidd (1952), once more Mr. Laughton

Captain Kidd and the Slave Girl (1954) with Anthony Dexter

Captain Kronos, Vampire Hunter (1972) with Horst Janson

Captain Lightfoot (1955) with Rock Hudson

Captain Nemo and the Underwater City (1970) with Robert Ryan

Captain Mephisto and the Transformation Machine (1945) with Wallace Grissell

Captain America (1944), starring Dick Purcell

The Adventures of Captain Marvel (1941), starring Tom
  Tyler
The Adventures of Captain Africa (1955), starring John
  Hart
Captain Midnight (1942), starring Dave O'Brien
Captain Video (1951) with Judd Holdren
Captain Newman, M.D. (1963) starring Gregory Peck
Captain Scarlett (1953) with Richard Greene
Captain Sindbad (1963) with Guy Williams
Captain Tugboat Annie (1945) with Jane Darwell
Captain Thunder (1931)

MORE . . . ROSES BY ANY
OTHER NAME

In the first book, we served up a number of actors who had changed their names to suit the whims of publicists. Here are several more:

Ramon Samaniegoes: Ramon Novarro
Julia Jean Turner: Lana Turner
Otto Linkenhelt: Elmo Lincoln
Rodolpho Alfonzo Rafaelo Pierre Filibert Guglielmi di
    Valentina d'Antonguollo: Rudolph Valentino
Mel Kaminsky: Mel Brooks
Isidore Itzkowitz: Eddie Cantor
Ernest Brimmer: Richard Dix
Bela Blasko: Bela Lugosi
Richard Jenkins: Richard Burton

PAYING THEIR DUES

Jobs held by actors before they decided upon performing for a living:

Robert Ryan: ranch hand
Boris Karloff: farm hand
Errol Flynn: overseer at a tobacco plantation
Kirk Douglas: janitor
Burt Lancaster: circus acrobat
Clifton Webb: dancing teacher
Omar Sharif: timber merchant
Oliver Reed: strip-joint bouncer
Gregory Peck: truck driver
Peter O'Toole: journalist
David Niven: bartender
Marilyn Monroe: munitions worker
Robert Mitchum: coal miner
Steve McQueen: carnival barker
Walter Matthau: basketball coach
Lee Marvin: plumber
Gene Kelly: bricklayer
Danny Kaye: insurance salesperson
Rock Hudson: postal carrier
James Garner: gas-station attendant
Glenn Ford: bus driver
Peter Finch: waiter
Clint Eastwood: lifeguard
Joseph Cotton: newspaper ad salesperson
Jeff Chandler: restaurant cashier
Yul Brynner: guitarist
Marlon Brando: ditchdigger
Carroll Baker: magician's aide

PAYING THEIR DUES (continued)

Sean Connery: undertaker
Dustin Hoffman: typist
Peter Lorre: bank teller
Kim Novak: elevator operator
Dick Van Dyke: ad-agency account executive

ALMA MATER

Colleges of the stars:

Warren Beatty: Northwestern
Yul Brynner: Sorbonne
Richard Burton: Oxford
James Coburn: USC
James Dean: UCLA
José Ferrer: Princeton
Rex Harrison: Liverpool College
Charlton Heston: Northwestern
William Holden: Pasadena Junior College
Burt Lancaster: NYU
Jayne Mansfield: UCLA
Paul Newman: Kenyon College (Ohio)
Gregory Peck: San Diego State College
George Peppard: Purdue
Vincent Price: Yale
Robert Redford: University of Colorado
Cliff Robertson: Antioch
Eva Marie Saint: University of Ohio
George C. Scott: University of Missouri
George Segal: Columbia University
Jon Voight: Catholic University of America (Washington, D.C.)
Cornel Wilde: Columbia University

LOVE-HATE

Highly lauded films which flopped at the box office:

Fame (1980): this Oscar-winning story of teens in a high school for the arts had one of its musical numbers on the top-ten charts—yet still failed.

Will Penny (1968): Charlton Heston's finest non-Biblical role, and a literate western about an aging cowboy.

The Conversation (1974): Gene Hackman starred, Francis Ford Coppola directed, and no one went to see this brooding, depressing story of a surveillance man who becomes emotionally involved in his case.

Atlantic City (1981): Burt Lancaster's best performance in years, as an aged bookie who makes a dramatic comeback in crime. A multiple award-winner which never found an audience.

J. W. Coop (1972): Cliff Robertson wrote, starred in, and directed this lauded story of a would-be rodeo champion; downbeat and beyond the experience of the average theatergoer, it failed.

Intolerance (1916): D. W. Griffith's condemnation of intolerance through the ages, based on his personal experience with resentment of his controversial blockbuster *Birth of a Nation* (1915). Produced at a then-record sum of $2 million, it was perhaps the greatest failure in film history, destroying Griffith's career. It is, withal, one of the most magnificent and engrossing films ever made.

Touch of Evil (1958): Charlton Heston starred in this Orson Welles picture, one of the director's greatest. Dark, evil, seedy, and brilliant, it failed for all of those reasons.

LOVE-HATE (continued)

Mean Streets (1973): Early Robert DeNiro film, a gritty drama of low life and crime, directed by Martin Scorsese. Popular in urban areas, the film's milieu, though not the stuff of which popular films are made.

Portrait of Jennie (1948); admired in its time, though more so now, this $4 million fantasy of Joseph Cotton's love for a dead woman was too ephemeral for mass appeal.

Charlie Bubbles (1968): Albert Finney's obscure, symbol-ridden film about a bored author co-starred newcomer Liza Minnelli. The miasma of bored artist and rich English setting made it a film of limited appeal.

The Sugarland Express (1974): Steven Spielberg *(Jaws)* directed Goldie Hawn in this, his first feature, about a couple trying to kidnap their own baby.

The Shootist (1976): John Wayne's last film, about a cancer-plagued gunman, earned him some of his finest reviews. The well-known fact of life imitating art may have put many people off.

Movies slammed by the critics, but heavy grossers just the same:

Every Which Way but Loose (1978): Clint Eastwood and Clyde the orangutan in an inarguably terrible picture which went on to become a huge hit and inspired a sequel, *Any Which Way You Can* (1980)

Stir Crazy (1980): This Richard Pryor/Gene Wilder comedy received some of the worst reviews in history and became the biggest success of the Xmas season. A sequel is in the works.

Clash of the Titans (1981) and *Excalibur* (1981): Very few critics had anything kind to say about these two fantasies, one the legend of the Greek hero Perseus and the other about King Arthur. Both made over $30 million in the United States alone, while the highly praised *Dragonslayer* went down the drain that same year.

Airport 1975 (1974): The first of the sequels to *Airport* (1970) was panned and made a fortune—not as much as the first, but in the $30 million range. *Airport 1975* was the best of the sequels, with *Airport 1977* (1976) and *Airport 1980* (1979) not only worse, but the latter actually failing to recoup its cost.

Moonraker (1979): The roundly panned eleventh James Bond film—yet, due to the nonstop and spectacular action scenes, the most successful of them all. The twelfth film, *For Your Eyes Only* (1981) received the best Bond notices in years, but didn't come close to matching the dimensions of the *Moonraker* cache.

Maniac (1980): Shot for $400,000, it made that much money in its first half-day of release. A vividly brutal tale, it was trashed by everyone, and a runaway hit. (Five minutes of the film's negative were lost in the lab; no one seemed to notice the gap in the film!)

Caligula (1979): *Penthouse* Magazine's hard-core version of the lunatic emperor's rule, with explicit sex and gore. Only *Penthouse* gave the film favorable press—but that was enough. At an average of $7.50 per ticket, the $17 million film quickly turned a profit.

Cleopatra (1963): Roundly panned, this superepic nonetheless had the public sufficiently intrigued by Liz and Dick to draw a massive audience. A huge hit by ordinary standards, the film grossed barely enough to break even after its $40 million cost.

WRITTEN BY THE STARS, CHAPTER TWO

In the first *Signet Book of Movie Lists*, we served up thirty-eight autobiographical works penned by actors themselves. In the three years since that list was compiled, other volumes have appeared:

Shelley, Also Known as Shirley by Shelley Winters
This Life by Sidney Poitier
My Story by Ingrid Bergman
Swanson by Swanson by Gloria Swanson
Lana Turner by Lana Turner
Ordeal by Linda Lovelace
An Actor and His Time by John Gielgud
True Britt by Britt Ekland
Please Don't Shoot My Dog by Jackie Cooper
A Hundred Different Lives by Raymond Massey
Nostalgia Isn't What It Used to Be by Simone Signoret
Bittersweet by Susan Strasberg
Up in the Clouds, Gentlemen, Please by John Mills
Sparks Fly Upward by Stewart Granger
Viveka . . . Viveca by Viveca Lindfors
My Side and *An Open Book* by Ruth Gordon
Topol by Topol

UNCA WALT

We all remember the famous films made by the Walt Disney Studios—the classic cartoons and live-action features which are released every seven or so years and seem as fresh as ever. But the studio has made other films which hardly ever surface, save as an occasional two-parter on the Disney TV show. Do you remember:

Bon Voyage (1962): the "adult" Disney film, about Fred MacMurray and family visiting France

Moon Pilot (1962): Tom Tryon as an astronaut, encountering an alien lady on earth

Toby Tyler (1960): Kevin Corcoran in the circus

Third Man on the Mountain (1959): Michael Rennie scales the Matterhorn in a forgotten Disney gem

The Three Lives of Thomasina (1964): Patrick McGoohan and a pussycat

The Happiest Millionaire (1967): a justly ignored musical with Tommy Steele and Fred MacMurray

Tonka (1958): Indian Sal Mineo and his horse, plus General Custer

The Boatniks (1970): Robert Morse in the Coast Guard

Blackbeard's Ghost (1967): Peter Ustinov as the pirate, Dean Jones as his confidant

Island at the Top of the World (1974): David Hartman ill-at-ease ballooning upon a civilization of Vikings at the pole

Saludos Amigos (1943): combination live-action and animated feature as Donald Duck and some Disney employees travel through South America

So Dear to My Heart (1949): turn-of-the-century drama of a boy and his sheep

The Adventures of Ichabod and Mr. Toad (1949): an ignored Disney feature, actually two featurettes: *The Legend of Sleepy Hollow* and *The Wind in the Willows*. Notable primarily for Ichabod Crane's flight from the Headless Horseman, which is among the finest animation the studio has ever produced

Perri the Flying Squirrel (1957): a beautiful "docudrama" about the furry figure

ABOUT THE AUTHOR

JEFF ROVIN, a workaholic and confirmed movie fan, now in his mid-twenties, was born in Brooklyn and raised on Long Island. After two years in college he dropped out to enter the field of publishing, working as a comic-book editor and even writing a romance column. His first book, *A Pictorial History of Science Fiction Films,* was followed by twelve others, including *The UFO Movie Quiz Book, The Superhero Movie & TV Quiz Book, Count Dracula's Vampire Quiz Book,* the last three in Signet paperback; *The Films of Charlton Heston, The Great Television Series,* and others. He is a frequent guest lecturer, speaking on science fiction, films, and movie effects, writes a column for *Analog* magazine, and articles for *Ladies Home Journal.*